GW01311795

GUY WILSON CREATING GOLF EXCELLENCE

The Genesis of Lydia Ko & More Stars

Bruce Miller

Cover by Queen Graphics. Cover picture and title page picture courtesy of Guy Wilson. Other pictures, and illustrations are from Creative Commons unless otherwise indicated.

ISBN: 978-1-99-104819-6 (Ingram Spark Paperback)

ISBN: 978-1-99-104820-2 (Ingram Spark Paperback – Color Edition)

ISBN: 978-1-99-104821-9 (Ingram Spark Hardcover)

ISBN: 978-1-99-104822-6 (Ingram Spark Hardcover-Color Edition)

ISBN: 9798389027619 (KDP Paperback)

ISBN: 9798389027909 (KDP Hardcover)

ISBN 9798389569430 (KDP Paperback - Color Edition)

ISBN 9798389569799 (KDP Hardcover – Color Edition)

Dedication

To all the fascinating people of all ages who may have an interest in golf and want to play your best game.

To those just starting or who have played golf all their life.

To those who have given it up or thinking about giving it up and to those getting back into the game we all enjoy.

To those who are trying to break 100 or 70.

To those who just want to socialize and have fun enjoying the sport.

And especially to those who want to learn more about an exceptional golf instructor and his ingenious style, guidance, attitude, humor, and all of that combined with a high IQ and high EQ which he uses to guide golfers both young and old on a wonderful journey to the top of their game.

Acknowledgments

Many thanks to Guy Wilson, Craig Dixon, Sir John Key, David Niethe, Michael Hendry, Gregg Thorpe, Mark and Sandie Jennins, and all the other great people who gave their time for interviews for this amazing story of the creative nature and insightful coaching of Guy Wilson and the positive results he produces.

So many busy and extraordinary people went out of their way to talk about Guy and his highly intelligent, humorous, and understanding nature, and his coaching of Lydia Ko and introducing and guiding her into the world of golf and the many other stars Guy created.

As I got to know Guy, I now better understand why they all gave their time to talk about this selfless and giving man.

Foreword by Sir John Key

Guy deserves the recognition he gets when it comes to teaching. As talented as the likes of Lydia Ko undoubtedly is, it was through the years of their partnership combined with hard work and teaching that I believe allowed her to become the world champion she is.

He is an outstanding coach because he can combine extreme knowledge of the game with a personalized approach to improvement. He doesn't apply the same prescription to every golfer. Whilst doing this, it's always mixed with humour, encouragement, and the power of positive thinking.

Guy immediately understood the many ingrained faults in my swing and set about attempting to change them. Along the way, he has set realistic goals and used technology and banter to reach our shared objectives.

His ability to text late at night is outstanding and I can only put this down to the understanding and forbearance of his wife Abby who everyone knows is the rock in the relationship.

Guy has a dogged determination to ensure his clients maximize their abilities. Lessons are challenging but fun.

Away from my engagement over the years, I've witnessed firsthand him teaching young people to play. He is patient, and fun and they love him.

-- Sir John Phillip Key GNZM, 38th Prime Minister of New Zealand (2008 to 2016), HCP 7.

Sir John Philip Key

By the way, on December 9th, 2022, Sir John scored a hole-in-one playing in the "Chasing the Fox" at Royal Auckland and Grange Golf Club to raise funds for The Make-a-Wish Foundation. Sir John hit a fade with a fairway metal on a long par 3 that rolled into the hole!

John remarked, "I saw it hit the green and heard everyone make quite a bit of noise, but I didn't even consider it would go in the hole. So, I just leant over to pick up my tee out of the ground.

Every golfer dreams of getting a hole-in-one and I'd been close on several occasions, so I got to the point where I thought I'd probably never get one."

Sir John received congratulations from around the world. He now joins the ranks of many other former country leaders who have had holes-in-one such as President Dwight D. Eisenhower, [1] President Gerald Ford, [2] and George W. Bush. [3]

"Teaching children is an accomplishment. Getting children excited about learning is an achievement."

"And, if we are truly effective teachers, then we are creating autonomous, independent, and self-directed learners, not just successful test-takers."

-- Robert John Meehan

Contents

Introduction

"All big things come from small beginnings. The seed of every habit is a single, tiny decision. But as that decision is repeated, a habit sprouts and grows stronger. Roots entrench themselves and branches grow."

— James Clear, excerpt from Atomic Habits

Small beginnings can lead to amazing achievements if you have a strong foundation. The game of golf is played by millions, young and old, and only a very few ever excelled at golf at such an early age as Lydia Ko.

Under Guy's guidance and coaching, Lydia, at age 13, won the 2011 Australian Women's Strokeplay Championship over last year's champion, Cecilia Cho (who Guy also coached later when Cecilia played the Korean PGA Tour). By the way, I use the word "guidance" since Guy not only coaches golf but also guides his unknowing students on the best paths to take in the massive golf world to best achieve their goals playing as an amateur or professionally at the highest levels.

The next year, at the age of 14, Lydia won the Women's New South Wales Open on WPGA Tour of Australasia, formerly known as the ALPG Tour, and was one of the youngest persons ever, male or female to win a *professional* golf event – and that's earlier than Jack or Tiger.

It didn't stop there. At the age of 15, she won the 2012 Canadian Women's Open on the LPGA Tour setting a record for the youngest golfer ever (15 years and 4 months) to win an event on the LPGA tour. [4] And she won that tournament again the following year. [5]

Lydia has been called "The Girl Wonder of Golf." [6] Tiger even told Lydia she was a better golfer at 15 than he was. [7]

The roots and foundation that Guy Wilson established for her have sprouted and continue to grow stronger.

At the end of 2022, she's ranked the No. 1 woman golfer in the world for the second time in her record-breaking career. She was the leading money winner on the LPGA Tour ($4.3 million), the winner of the 2022 Vare Trophy (lowest scoring average), and the 2022 Rolex Player of the Year for the second time in her unbelievable career.

Korean-born, Lydia didn't speak much English when her mother, Tina Hyon (Korean married women keep their maiden name) walked her into the Pupuke Golf Club north of Auckland and met Guy for the first time.

Guy was in the pro shop when Tina asked him about giving little Lydia lessons. Lydia was around 5 or 6 years old and could barely see over the counter.

Guy agreed to teach Lydia her first-ever golf lessons, and over the next 11 years, he guided and coached Lydia to the world stage.

Gregg Thorpe is Golf New Zealand's high-performance manager who handles top-performing golfers and has known Guy for years due to Guy continuing to produce high-performing players. Golf New Zealand is NZ's governing body, and the high-performance manager guides talented NZ players and helps them compete overseas.

Gregg explained, "Coaches are special people. They give so much of themselves. And often they are doing that without necessarily putting their career or even their income at the forefront of that. The first thing for them is to provide a happy safe environment for the athlete to succeed in.

"For example, there are coaches who are just the opposite. Those who have an authoritarian approach where they say for example, 'You do it my way, and this is going to be how it is, and you're not going to like it but you're going to be good.'

"What separates Guy from other coaches who are standing on the range and delivering just instruction -- and that, of course, is part of coaching -- is this: to look into the person's eyes and start to understand and learn about the student.

"True golf coaching is far more about students who are human beings and inspiring them. It's knowing when they are down and bringing them back up. It's knowing when it's time to push and when not to push. It's knowing when they're up... and bringing them back down – and being aware and knowing that golf is a long journey."

"What separates Guy from other coaches… is this: to look into the person's eyes and start to understand and learn about the student. True golf coaching is far more about students who are human beings and inspiring them."

You will discover in this book how Guy created, coached, and guided Lydia and many other stars. You will learn about his style of coaching, guidance, attitude, humor, and natural ability to guide young as well as older golfers.

You will learn how to improve your game and how to help your children, loved ones, friends, and associates to find the right golf coach for them so they can easier learn and enjoy what can be a difficult and frustrating game.

You will learn how Guy and the team at the Institute of Golf are continuing to create high-performance players, getting major university golf scholarships, winning golf tournaments, becoming champions at the highest levels in golf, and much more.

Keeping Promises.

"People with good intentions make promises, but people with good character keep them."

-- Anon.

Golf coaches normally don't find themselves standing on a small rectangular wooden platform almost 15 stories high above a flowing river with an elastic cord tied around their ankles. He promised Lydia if she won that tournament, he would do a bungy jump.

Lydia won.

He came here to the Kawarau Bridge Bungy Center for a cocktail evening on a Wednesday night sponsored by AJ Hackett. He promised Olympic rowing gold medalist Mahe Drysdale to caddy for him here at the 2013 NZ PGA Championship Pro-Am taking place the next morning at the nearby Hills Golf Course. Lydia was also there encouraging her wonderful instructor to do the jump.

He knew about possible injuries. Eye hemorrhaging, intense spinal pressures, compression fractures, broken bones, herniated discs, and if his neck somehow got tangled only for a short time in the stretching elastic cord, death would almost instantly occur.

But here he was on a small rectangular wooden platform looking down at the recovery boat in the narrow river far below and the spectators nearby, while half-listening to the attendant about what he was about to do.

Kawarau Bridge Bungy Center (Picture courtesy of Guy Wilson)

He was surprised at how the drop looked a lot deeper standing there than it looked from afar. Mahe Drysdale promised he would do a jump after Guy, so that would be something to talk about.

But no backing out now! Shaking off his anxiousness, he knew a promise is a promise – something he always kept. He'd committed himself to do this jump like he permanently commits to a long golf shot to a tiny well-bunkered green.

He inched his way to the end of the platform.

With his heart pounding, mind racing and a perspiring hand slipping off the metal support, his mind went blank, then he took off!

(Picture courtesy of Guy Wilson)

His body exploded with adrenaline! He'd been on roller coasters, but this was highly more intense. Strongest building G force he'd ever felt as wind gushed around him, into his face, and deep into his eyes as he looked down at the river!

Time stood still as jagged cliffsides rushed by. The small bits of food he'd eaten felt like rocks in his stomach. Strangely, the cord wasn't easing as the waters below rushed toward him. Tension began building in his lower back and neck.

(Picture courtesy of Guy Wilson)

Then he felt the cord slowing him down easing the gravitation forces as the cord stretched. The waters below were approaching more slowly now, and he could smell the crystal-clear waters wondering if he'd get a bit wet.

Trusting the cord seemed a bit like trusting a golf club. You don't think about it more once you decided what club you want to hit. Just let it do its job.

The cord was doing its job! His stomach was still sinking as a strong feeling of relief enveloped him.

Then, up and up he went!

(Picture courtesy of Guy Wilson)

Swaying and swinging from the cord, he felt himself slow from the 160 kph free fall. 'I did it feelings' entered his consciousness.

He was thankful for this exceptional adventure and for Lydia urging him to do this.

Hanging upside down, he waited for the bouncing to lessen. Blood started collecting at the top of his head. He dangled and swayed helplessly, then he felt himself being lowered into the boat below.

(Picture courtesy of Guy Wilson)

It was wonderful to step out of his comfort zone now and then, he thought. Now, where is that boat?

As the boat collected him, he knew he now had an amazing lifetime memory.

As they unhitched the harness, he gave a wave to those above and then wondered what in the world he would promise if Lydia conquered her next challenge.

And then he started thinking and planning about more motivational things he would promise her in the future.

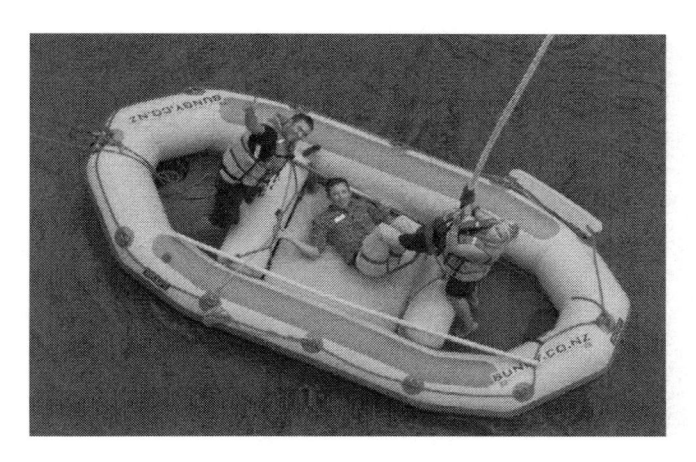

(Picture courtesy of Guy Wilson)

"A commitment is what transforms a promise into reality."

-- Abraham Lincoln

IQ, EQ, and Comedy

"It is the supreme art of the teacher to awaken joy in creative expression and knowledge."

-- Albert Einstein

When Lydia was around 8 years old, Guy arranged for her and her parents to see David Niethe a high-performance sports coach. David helped Lydia with the mental game and met with her and her parents about every month when they started, then less frequently as Lydia progressed.

When I walked into his well-appointed office, I noticed many pictures of sports celebrities hanging on the walls.

There was a large picture of Lydia Ko showing her hitting a tee shot in front of a large crowd of spectators and signed by her with a big "Thank you!" and a personal message to David.

There was also a signed autographed poster of renowned World Champion Mixed Martial Artist, Israel Adesanya in full fighting gear signed by Israel likewise thanking David and a personal message to him.

There were more pictures of many sports stars with thank you messages from major rugby stars, and many other notables from a wide range of world sports.

I sat down on a large leather couch across from David and after exchanging brief introductions, I learned he has degrees in neurolinguistic programming and hypnotherapy. He competed in New Zealand's World's Strongest Man competitions and has a very interesting and highly successful life.

I asked him his opinion of Guy Wilson.

"I think one of the keys to Guy is first his passion for coaching. He has a love for people.

"Secondly, he is not one to conform to rules. Guy is Guy. He has his own style and is very intelligent and keen to learn.

"But one of the keys to the relationship that I observed was that as Lydia developed her understanding of the fundamentals of golf, she would be constantly asking Guy questions, and Guy would not be forthcoming with answers.

"Instead, he would say, "Work it out," or "Tell me what you think." He was developing her golfing understanding, and he challenged her to take absolute responsibility for understanding why he was doing that."

That reminded me of what industrialist and famous teacher Clay Bedford once said, *"You can teach a student a lesson for a day; but if you can teach him to learn by creating curiosity, he will continue the learning process as long as he lives."*

David continued, "You know Lydia has a golf intellect that fundamentally was developed by Guy. He is incredibly humanistic. What do you think?"

I replied that I thought Guy is certainly highly intelligent and had exceptional Emotional Intelligence -- a high EQ.

"He has a combination of both. He has a high IQ and a high EQ. And he uses them. In my view, to develop champions, you can't have one or the other. Champions need an exceptional coach who has EQ and IQ."

I certainly agreed with that, and David continued.

"Another talent he has that combines with his IQ and EQ is comedy. He has a spontaneous and creative sense of humor. He can engage and disengage. He will get serious and then he will joke around.

"And here's the thing because he jokes around and gets serious, he creates this variety. It's like for the clients, which of the two would you prefer?

"Tell me, how do you feel when you make the many hour drive to Auckland?"

"Tired," I said.

"How do you feel when come off a roller coaster ride?"

I'd been on the screaming rollercoasters in Orlando and Tampa and said, "Excited! It's all an adrenaline rush!"

"What Guy has is this ability to make golf practice and playing the game exciting and having the desire to become the best version of yourself. He is a master of that.

"He's developed Bohyun Park, Fiona Xu, Ruoning (Judy) Yin, and more. Let me tell you something. It's about baking a cake.

"When you were a kid did your grandma make something like a great cake that you and the rest absolutely loved?

"And obviously, grandma is not going to be around forever. So, what do you need?"

I wasn't sure what he was getting at and before I could answer I heard –

"You need a recipe!! Guy has the recipe to constantly make more cake. Do you know what I mean? When you create an environment with golf practice areas to learn the craft of golf, learning golf becomes the most exciting thing these kids enjoy.

"They go to school, then they come to golf with Guy, and they say I don't want to go back to school. I just want to be here. Because there's variety, there's fun – Guy creates an environment for excellence."

I agreed Guy certainly does that. I asked David about Guy giving his students incentives he creates to perform well. I explained that Guy would tell Lydia that if she was successful in an event, he would jump in a lake with his clothes on, or he would do a bungy jump, and so on.

I also read Guy promised Lydia he would propose to his girlfriend, Abby whom he was dating for some time when Lydia became the World's No. 1 female golfer.

And, when Lydia became World No. 1, he proposed to Abby and married her. Lydia sent them her warm congratulations!

"Yes. He gave Lydia incentives and she loved that! That was a win–win for both.

"But here's the interesting thing as far as that philosophy goes. The only true way it will go well is to help others get what they want. Guy is a prime example of a person who has that philosophy. He genuinely wants to see you succeed."

"The only true way it will go well is to help others get what they want. Guy is a prime example of a person who has that philosophy. He genuinely wants to see you succeed."

Golf NZ High-performance manager Gregg Thorpe told more of his personal views. "Guy was very good at getting the most out of Lydia's time during practice sessions. It was never about hitting ball after ball. It was about challenging her and her decision-making and playing the game, not just ingraining techniques.

"In my opinion, he's a great coach because of the environment that he provides. Guy is naturally a competitive person. He does it in a playful way with players. He creates an environment where they can enjoy doing hard work. It may not necessarily be fun, but it appears they really enjoy it.

"There are moments in time where his students will be grinding away on the range and maybe no one else there to see it but they will be having a joke together. They'll be smiling. And someone will joke, and they'll be laughing for a moment then they'll get back to work. They'll do the work that needs to be done. And I think it's a lovely blend."

Having fun while working hard certainly seems to be an enjoyable and successful journey. As I learned more about Guy, I found he has an effortless natural humor and keeps children highly entertained and eager to practice more.

For example, I learned when Guy and 7-year-old Lydia were practicing on the Pupuke golf course, they would stop on the fairway 60 meters from the hole and play "closest to the pin."

If Lydia hit a bad shot, Guy wouldn't comment about her bad shot. He'd confidently and silently step up to the ball and go through his highly professional pre-shot routine. Then he'd say something like, "This is going to be an instant win," and then whiff it or chunk it (on purpose) and Lydia would roar with laughter!

Studies have confirmed entertainment and laughter do enhance learning. Scholars have shown laughter enhances learning and boosts retention. [8] Laughing causes the brain to release endorphins that naturally relax the body and enhance focus and relaxation, create a sense of well-being, and much more. [9]

If Lydia hit a bad shot, Guy wouldn't comment about her bad shot. He'd confidently and silently step up to the ball and go through his highly professional pre-shot routine. Then he'd say something like, "This is going to be an instant win," and then whiff it or chunk it (on purpose) and Lydia would roar with laughter!

Researchers Lawrence Robinson, Melinda Smith, M.A., and Jeanne Segal, Ph.D., wrote, "Laughter is strong medicine. Laughter strengthens your immune system, boosts the mind and mood, and protects you from the harmful effects of tension. Nothing works faster or more dependably to bring your mind and body back into balance than a good laugh." [10]

And bringing your mind and body back into balance makes it easier for any golfer or child to learn a sometimes very difficult adult sport. As Walt Disney said, "Laughter is no enemy to learning."

The Genesis of High Performance – Building a Solid Foundation

"Building a solid foundation in the early years of a child's life will not only help someone reach their reach their full potential but will also result in better societies as a whole."

— Novak Djokovic

Like Lydia Ko, Guy started playing golf at an early age learning to see the sport through a child's eye. Guy and his brother played at the Pupuke Golf Course located north of Auckland every day after school. They routinely competed against each other -- who could shoot the lowest score, make the longest putt, chip the closest, and so on.

"I walked to the course every day after school. Golf was in a sense a babysitter for my older brother, Tay, and me while Dad worked until 5 pm. It was also our social network, and all our friends were there."

During high school, the Wilson brothers became junior members of the course. Tay later moved to Melbourne to pursue a greenkeeping career and now is the superintendent at the private Kooringal golf course -- one of Melbourne's most prestigious clubs.

When Lydia was competing in Australia in amateur competitions, Tay was instrumental in arranging accommodations, practice rounds, and other details for Lydia and her parents.

As years went by at Pupuke, Guy started working in the pro shop and found he enjoyed the golf environment and eventually came to know all the members. He was well-liked by all because of his good nature and considerateness.

Mark Jennins, a former board member at the club told me, "I was a terrible bunker player. So, I was at the course practicing my bunker shots. Guy was coaching nearby and noticed what I was doing. He must have thought to himself, *'Mark's got it all wrong.'*

"So, he comes across the course and tells me, 'Mark, with a bunker shot you've got to play a full shot.'"

"Honestly, right as we speak, I am today a very good bunker player after that. Great advice at no charge. He just came across the course to me and it made a big difference and that is just the sort of person he is."

Guy played competitively against high-ranking amateurs and professionals but found he enjoyed the golf environment and coaching. The pro shop scene appealed to him. So much so, after he graduated high school, he decided to make golf his career and began his 3-year NZPGA apprenticeship at Pupuke.

The day Tina and her daughter, Lydia walked through the front door of the pro shop Guy didn't think there was anything highly extraordinary about it. It wasn't unusual in 2002 for a Korean woman to bring her daughter in to learn golf – except that little Lydia could barely see over the counter.

It did seem a bit unusual to him for such a little girl to take lessons. And at that time in New Zealand, little girls didn't play golf at all.

He learned from Tina they recently moved in just across the road. Tina and her husband Gil-Hong Ko came from Jeju Island, Korea, and moved to Australia where they visited with Lydia's aunt, Insook Hyon, who took Lydia to a driving range and gave her two golf clubs, a 7 iron, and a putter. Lydia overall was very inexperienced as any 5 or 6-year-old would be.

Tina wanted to sign her daughter up for 3 lessons a week and Guy was happy to do that.

Tina and Gil Hong were like any other parents who want to get their children to learn a skill whether it be piano or violin lessons, tennis or golf, etc. Taking lessons and learning a skill teaches a child to develop memory skills, concentration, coordination, self-discipline, confidence, and other important things we all need in our lives.

Little Lydia seemed to enjoy the driving range with her aunt. At that time, teenage Korean Inbee Park was having success playing competitive golf and was admired by many. But no one had any idea that Lydia would be so good.

Tina and Gil Hong were considering moving to either Canada or New Zealand and chose New Zealand since it had a better climate.

Lydia spoke little English, and Guy didn't speak Korean, but somehow, they got along exceptionally well. Guy said, "The lessons were 45 minutes and there's not much you can do with a little child who doesn't understand you very well trying to hit a golf ball with clubs that were way too big for her."

"She would laugh a lot and at that age she really didn't know a lot about why she was doing it. It was just one activity to another activity in her mind. And at that young age, there isn't much motivation. She didn't realize at that age that if I shot a lower score, it would be better for me. She just tried to hit the golf ball and she didn't really consider much more at that stage."

But how can anyone teach a little 5–6-year-old child the puzzling game of golf? And how do you overcome a small child's short attention span and endless curiosity?

Guy explained, "It's difficult with children to keep them interested so you must make it fun. I made little games up, so it wasn't so one-dimensional.

"Going through the ups and downs of golf at any level, the golfer needs to enjoy it because it is going to challenge you. And if you don't enjoy it, it will beat you every time. And that's what I try to instill into children and anyone I teach."

Guy knew it was important for her to be relaxed. "I spent the most part of little Lydia's first lesson just getting Lydia to be comfortable around a stranger."

He took her to the chipping green and putting green and focused on just getting Lydia comfortable with it all.

Many people say Guy has an exceptionally high Emotional Intelligence (EQ) as well as a high IQ. When you combine high EQ & IQ with lots of natural humor and creativity, that gives his students many factors of enjoyment and Guy is known for his natural clever humor.

As mentioned before, laughter does help learning. The George Lucas Educational Foundation supported research that has proven that laughter makes learning much easier and boosts retention. [11]

The study found, "Humor activates the brain's dopamine reward system, stimulating goal-oriented motivation and long-term memory, which means that humor does improve retention in students of all ages." [12]

So, what do you do with a small child to teach her golf?

Guy created ways for little Lydia to experience success – like just simply trying to get the ball into the hole, small competitions filled with humor, all designed so that Lydia could experience laughter, joy, and those great "I did it feelings."

He varied the games using different slopes on the green, chipping competitions, and more keeping it all fun and enjoyable.

As the lessons progressed, Lydia's mom saw how much Lydia was enjoying herself and how Guy and Lydia were getting along so well and having lots of laughs.

Guy explained, "Lydia had a nice natural ability but couldn't hit the ball very far at such a young age. So, I played golf games with her around the green to see who could hit the ball in the hole first, arranged different types of putts, short putts, long putts, who could get the ball closest to the hole, uphill putts, downhill putts, and more."

They'd play more games such as chipping around the green seeing "who could chip it closest."

Lydia took to the idea quickly of getting the ball to the pin and it would make anyone smile to see little Lydia so focused staring down the pins. And the fun, learning, retention, and skills continued for the next 11 years as she developed more through Guy's instruction.

So why did Guy believe in making it all fun?

"I believe that if a child wants to have a lot of fun, then go for it -- as long as it's safe. That is, as long as you don't hurt yourself or injure anybody, then it's best to make it as much fun as possible for them so they want to come back.

"The reason for this is that those young kids – they're the ones to say, 'Can I go to golf again?' Or 'can I go practice', or 'can we go see the coach again?' Then that's a win when parents aren't pushing the kids.

"You can't teach golf in one single lesson. It is a journey, and a skilled coach must make it an enjoyable journey, or they will lose interest."

He added, "Even as a little girl, Lydia had a great instinct and feel around the greens and that's probably why she has such a great short game."

That certainly is true today. LPGA Statistics for 2022 show Lydia led the scoring average (68.988), bogey-free rounds (17), and top-10 percentage (63.6%). [13]

Guy's teaching methods work very well for children and teens as very few lose interest when Guy teaches them at the Institute of Golf (IOG).

Even if a student does not make it to the college level or as a professional, Guy has found that if the enjoyment of the game continues for a child through the teen years (which it usually does at IOG), they graduate High School at a very high skill level compared to their friends who might be just starting to take an interest in golf and that by itself creates a lot of enjoyment, satisfaction, and self-confidence.

The sport also creates closer family ties when a family plays golf together.

Those long clubs. "Lydia had a set of clubs that were way too long for her, and she was trying to play golf with those long clubs. At the time when she began to learn how to properly strike a golf ball, there was no such thing as junior golf clubs in New Zealand.

"So, I made a set for her by cutting down the shafts and putting grips on them, but they were not balanced and nothing like what you can get nowadays.

"These days you can get clubs for 3 or 4-year-olds that are light as a feather and perfectly balanced. In Lydia's learning days we were making do with what we could do."

Using women's clubs from one of the major brands, Guy shortened the shafts, colored them, and put different brightly colored grips all adding to the enjoyment and novelty of the lessons.

Her eyes lit up when she first saw her very specially made, multi-colored clubs with funny children's headcovers, and more funny features all adding enjoyment for a little girl.

Lydia gradually learned the golf swing. "When we first started, she was 5 or 6 years old, and I just let her swing away as children do as it's difficult to develop a golf swing at that young age. Also, a child has difficulty in understanding the technical part of golf. So, I concentrated on the enjoyment factor by improving the things she could do like chipping and putting."

Guy told me he didn't want Lydia to overhit or create more power than she physically could manage as the months went by. "That might have led to an injury or even a permanent injury."

Instead, he taught her the importance of tempo - having good rhythm and ball striking. But the main goal when she was a very small child was to always make it fun when she first learned the game.

The members of the club got used to seeing Lydia practicing with Guy. If those two weren't in their usual golf cart roaming for an empty place to practice on the course, they would see Guy carrying the clubs he made for her while Lydia practiced her cartwheels and skipped up and down the fairways.

Golf pro, Michael Hendry knows competitive golf having won several times on the PGA Tour Australia, the Japan Golf Tour, the New Zealand Open, the Indonesia Open on the Asian Tour, and others. "It's hard to think of anyone who has done a better job to take a 6-year-old kid and harness her talent and keep it focused – it's just remarkable! How can anyone keep a small child entertained with a sport that so many get frustrated with?

"I've watched Guy and Lydia. Guy has a remarkable ability, and it was masterful to see him find a way to make every practice session worthwhile. He would engineer each practice session to reach the goal he wanted to reach for that day.

"It's hard to think of anyone who has done a better job to take a 6-year-old kid and harness her talent and keep it focused – it's just remarkable! How can anyone keep a small child entertained with a sport that so many get frustrated with."

"On some days, Lydia like anyone had good days and bad days. Guy could read that better than anyone I've ever seen. If it was a bad day, he made it enjoyable and fun. He has a unique ability to flip the practice session around from a seriously bad day to a day filled with laughter. And no matter what the case – good day or bad day -- he would strive to manipulate her to achieve the goal for that day.

"And how he took a little girl who would skip and cartwheel down the fairways and harness her talent and turn her into the world champion she is today is certainly amazing!

"Guy was nominated for New Zealand's most prestigious sports achievement award, Coach of the Year at "The Halberg Awards", and in my view, he should have won it."

Michael Hendry 2012 NZ PGA Champion (Picture courtesy of Guy Wilson)

I asked Guy more about the practice sessions he created with little Lydia.

"Another and perhaps the most effective way of coaching a child is not so much on the range but on the golf course. We had to work around other members on the course and at times, find a spot on the course to have a challenge or a competition.

"We would shoot out to somewhere on the course and find a place. And driving a cart at the Pupuke GC is difficult since it is very sloped. So sloped that most of the time, you hit from either the bottom of the hill or hit down the hill. And for a child to hit up the hill is nearly impossible.

"As the lessons progressed, we worked on the techniques of the swing, and as I taught Lydia how to swing, she eventually learned it and I eventually had her doing a fully developed golf swing."

Guy also had her practicing shots that focused on hitting the ball to certain spots on the course or directly at the pin.

"That would be the basis of my coaching when she was very young. I would challenge her to hit certain shots and see whether she was able to do it.

"Pupuke is a very challenging course. The land changes and you had to be very strong to play golf around there. So, it is an easy place to fast track her learning of what a golf ball does when you hit it depending on the slopes and lies."

At that time, there weren't many other children playing or practicing golf at Pupuke. It was just herself, her mum or her father, and Guy. "There weren't many young girls playing at that time and socializing with other young girl golfers was difficult."

Lydia gradually improved as the lessons progressed and Lydia started showing a lot of talent. But Guy didn't have anyone to compare her. "She was around 7 and there weren't many other

7-year-olds playing golf at that time. She was enjoying it and we were having a lot of fun playing golf.

"At that time, there weren't many competitions for juniors and no milestones to measure her against other junior golfers."

So, for a while Guy competed with her to see if she could so to speak "beat the pro" by seeing who could score better on a golf hole. When they practiced competing on a hole and Lydia wasn't playing well, "I would just lighten the situation by purposely hitting bad shots himself. I would just hit a bad shot and she would roar with a laugh and wind up winning."

I asked Guy more about that. "We played a lot of games against each other and early in the game I would lose on purpose so she would feel more comfortable or feel like she's succeeding."

Lydia practiced at the Pupuke golf course regularly with her father Gil Hong and it was costly to play there without a membership. She also needed to establish a handicap.

So, Guy took it upon himself and asked the board to establish a special membership for her. He didn't want her to have to pay green fees as Lydia's family at that time weren't wealthy people. It was too expensive for Lydia's parents to pay for daily rounds of golf at Pupuke.

Lydia highly enjoyed golf and through Guy's efforts with the board at the Pupuke GC, Lydia was able to get a special membership for $100 per year which enabled her to establish a handicap.

Once she had a handicap, Guy was able to have her enter tournaments so they could measure her against other players.

Guy got her this special membership by asking the board to make a membership classification for young golfers like Lydia. The only other membership they had was a junior membership which started at age 12 and Lydia was 7.

Mark Jennins was a board member at Pupuke at the time. "It was a first for our club and probably a first for any club in New Zealand to have a little girl as a member. Everyone on the board knew her and we all liked Guy. She had been being taught by Guy for a couple a years or more and progressed very rapidly.

"I was on the board and Guy persuaded the board that Lydia should become a member. That was pretty much unheard of at that time. The youngest membership in New Zealand at that time began at age 10 and up." Mark Jennins said.

"The board gave Lydia special dispensation. And that would give Lydia a handicap and the ability to practice on the course without paying green fees."

With a special membership, Lydia could now practice as much as she wanted at the course and didn't have to pay green fees each time she played.

Lydia was now able to compete with other golfers. Guy arranged to have her play with much older golfers who were in their late teens as well as adult women and men.

Having an official handicap also allowed Lydia to join the North Harbour provincial golf team and compete against the other provincial teams in New Zealand and she did very well.

Her first handicap was 22. Guy explained, "It was hard to see at first that she was going to be exceptional since a 22 hcp isn't that remarkable but a bit mind-blowing for an 8-year-old girl."

Under Guy's coaching, her handicap went down. "Lydia was competing against adult women and Lydia would shoot 82 and which was amazing for an 8-year-old while the older woman would shoot around 75.

"They played from the ladies' tees in New Zealand since there was no such thing as Junior tees back then. She only learned about Junior tees in America. When she shot off the Junior tees in the US, she was able to shoot par or even under par. The Junior tees enabled Lydia to hit the driver and irons on par 4s and could reach the green in regulation.

"Later, when she was about 9, no matter what I did I could not win. I could not beat her because she was just too good, and I was shooting in the low to middle 70s."

Sandie Jennins, a prominent woman golfer at the club was also a talented golfer at a young age. Sandie went on to win numerous club championships and she helped around the club.

"Guy and Lydia were just gorgeous. Lydia was just lovely. They were just having fun and joked with each other and developing a strong older brother younger sister relationship.

"Lydia would also come up to me in the Starter's office with her father to practice regularly. Her father devoted a lot of time to her, and her parents were just lovely. Guy was a natural teacher who knew how to teach and handle young children way above the norm."

Sandie was a leading member of the provincial team for the North Harbour Province located just north of Auckland. She said, "I picked Lydia for the provincial team when she was ten years old. Her parents were wonderful."

"Guy was a natural teacher who knew how to teach and handle young children way above the norm."

"The other girls on the team were in their early 20s or older and gave Lydia lots of support. I would drive some of the girls and Lydia in a van to different tournaments and we had a great team spirit."

Sandie mentioned when Lydia would play a match against the older girls, "They would laugh that such a young girl would have such a low handicap. Then they would stop laughing when they saw Lydia play."

North Harbour Women's Golf Team -- Lydia is in the first row on the far-right
(Picture courtesy of Sandie Jennins)

I asked Guy for his thoughts about Lydia competing against much older golfers.

"It was my view that when she won tournaments at an early age, she felt very embarrassed just because she was so young. She was playing against adults. And perhaps a lot of the adults may not have been taking too kindly to this little girl coming here and beating them all.

"Lydia was also naturally very shy when she was just a little girl. It was difficult for her to be vocal since there weren't many children around - mostly adults - and it took her a couple of years to be comfortable where she was okay feeling it was right for her to be there."

How did she handle winning tournaments and matches?

"Lydia didn't enjoy the attention at first. In the beginning, she wasn't motivated to win. She just played her natural game. Accepting awards was something she gradually got better at but at first, she didn't enjoy all the attention. I'm sure you can understand since she was a little girl.

"Also, Korean people put a high value on honoring adults and teaching children to respect their elders. And Lydia was beating adults all the time. My impression was that she didn't feel comfortable doing that at first."

So how can a coach guide a child competing against adults and feel comfortable after beating them and not embarrassed?

"I would just be with her and support her so she would have a friend there during those uncomfortable times. And I would encourage her to talk about it. I might say, 'Hey this is fun! This is part of our journey by beating the pants off these older people and smiling while doing it.'

"And, slowly she became comfortable with it and people started recognizing her at Pupuke as that little girl who was practicing every day after school. They'd point her out and say, 'That's the little girl that just beat us.' Eventually, the members became more comfortable with it."

I told Guy that I've read Lydia is sincerely compassionate towards her competitors and at times even encourages them. That shows great sportsmanship, and she sets a wonderful example. What's your view on that?

"That is just the kind of person she is. Lydia is modest and humble. And that's why she didn't like the fanfare so much as she began beating low-handicap adult golfers. She wasn't one to say, 'Hey I'm really famous,' or seek more accolades.

"She wants other people to succeed. She wasn't like others that say, 'I am number one and I'm going to win!'"

David Niethe previously said to me, "Guy genuinely wants his students to succeed."

I thought Guy's own example of helping others to succeed surely influenced Lydia that way. Kids sometimes forget everything you teach them, but they certainly remember what kind of person you are, and that stayed with Lydia in my view.

It seems to me the average instructor narrates how to do something and a better than average instructor narrates and explains the fundamentals of golf.

Most of the top instructors who have years of experience also demonstrate and use technology to show students how to perform better. Guy goes beyond that by explaining things very well, demonstrates, uses technology, and by his example inspires and encourages students to enjoy the game as well. That, in my opinion, is highly conducive to learn it all much easier.

It also seems his purpose is to start the student's imagination on how to play better and enjoy it. He does that by looking into the student's heart and mind and determining how he can ignite a need in their spirit to learn more about the game.

Creating Enjoyable Practice Sessions

"The glory is being happy. The glory is not winning here or winning there. The glory is enjoying practicing, enjoy every day, enjoying working hard, trying to be a better player than before."

--Rafael Nadal

Lydia practicing at Gulf Harbour (Picture courtesy of Guy Wilson)

You don't always practice from easy positions!

Guy believes practicing doesn't mean you have to hit thousands of balls a week. Problem-solving is just as important when practicing and doing difficult shots makes the student feel much more comfortable when testing and developing difficult shot skills. It builds confidence.

Jack Nicklaus said, "Confidence is the most important single factor in this game, and no matter how great your natural talent, there is only one way to obtain and sustain it and that is practice."

New Zealand golf professional, Michael Hendry knows Guy and Lydia very well. "I've known Lydia since the moment she walked in the door at Pupuke. I was on the putting green at Pupuke that day.

"I've never seen anyone on the grind having a smile on their face the way Lydia did. And I put that down to Guy. What he achieved with Lydia was to make every single practice session relevant and enjoyable. I've never seen any other coach be able to instill the level of enjoyment into boring, repetitive, fatiguing practice the way Guy did. It was never a chore for her to spend hours on the driving range.

"Personally, I think that was more important in making her the golfer she is today is the fact that he made the time she spent practicing enjoyable – she was prepared to put the time in and never got sick of it. She just loved coming to golf – just loved it.

"What Guy did with her is still one of the most amazing pieces of coaching I've ever seen."

Lydia and Michael Hendry at IOG (Picture courtesy of Guy Wilson and IOG)

Guy explained, "At the time I helped Lydia, I thought that if I could get this little girl to that point in this lesson, then that was a win for me since I was unable at that time to spend all my time with her.

"The primary focus of a golfer is the time between the lessons – that's the valuable stuff. During lessons, if a coach makes it enjoyable for the student and he or she really and truly is enjoying it, they're eager to go and practice between the lessons."

I asked Guy his view of the general criticism when a young child is immersed in a sport and misses a normal childhood. Many feel children should have more balance when they're young. Missing a normal childhood with a lot of socialization among others your own age is a sacrifice. Lydia wanted to be an excellent golfer and said her parents taught her, "If you make a sacrifice, then something you want to achieve will come."

Children of course need to have fun growing up. Guy agreed. "Very young children need fun and enjoyment and that is the best journey for them – to enjoy it and show improvement."

That sounded like what philosopher, Carl Jung wrote, "The curriculum is not so much necessary raw material, but warmth is the vital element for the growing plant and for the soul of the child."

As I learned more about Guy, he is perceptive and caring with great insight and sensitivity to what children enjoy. I asked him about the days when Lydia might have not wanted to practice golf.

"There were times when I would find Lydia grinding away on the range hitting ball after ball before a lesson. So, before I start a lesson, I would turn on Korean pop-tunes, and lighten it all up.

"As Lydia progressed, I spent thousands and thousands of hours with her during lessons and at tournaments. And that made her junior golf competitions easier since I was there supporting and guiding her. I kept working with her and always tried to keep it fun. And Lydia's parents were very supportive.

"It is very different nowadays. In those days, Lydia didn't have many other girls who were 7- or 8-year-olds to socialize with about golf. It was lonely and not what it is nowadays.

"I'm not inclined to push students. If you want to have a lot of fun, then go for it as long as it's safe."

Guy not only made sure the children he coaches enjoy it but also challenges them. He uses his keen ability to "see the shot" and ingrained that in Lydia. He continues to challenge his students today to do the same.

Lydia would practice for 4-5 hours every day (weather permitting) after school. Most of her younger years were spent practicing at Pupuke GC. Guy would also arrange for her to play other courses for a change of scenery and diversity to enhance her practice sessions.

"We didn't want to miss the opportunities at the end of the day or during the weekend in daylight hours to practice and get a partnership with another golf club or golf facility. At that point she wasn't World No. 1. She was just an amazing athlete who was 8 or 9 years old.

"But I knew we needed variety in her practice and golf play. She couldn't afford to be a member at 3 or 4 courses, so I had to find other places, talk to the pro there, to help her get more experience playing."

As mentioned at the beginning of this book, Guy said it's hard to teach golf technicalities when a child is very young. He felt, "It was best to keep it simple then."

I asked Guy about how he taught Lydia the golf swing. "We were always working on her swing. Back in those days, there weren't the technical aids that you have today. I wanted to develop her with an efficient swing having a good rhythm and tempo that would last her for years and not cause injury to parts of her body by overstress.

"I used videos of other top LPGA tour players. There are a lot of efficient Korean golf swings with good tempo and rhythm."

So, you would work on building an efficient and lasting swing?

"Lydia didn't know much about a golf swing when she was very young, so we discussed swings a lot. I didn't want to teach her a crazy-looking swing that generates a lot of power since having a powerful swing may bring more inconsistencies with it.

"I also taught her how to work her way around the course, how the ball may react, and what sort of shot she should hit next. I wanted her "to see the shot" and have her thinking about how to hit the shot and make sure she was thinking about it the right way.

"Lydia didn't have a lot of years of experience to feed on. Teaching her these things made her a lot more confident. And I could see her confidence growing as the years of teaching went on."

Socrates wrote, "I cannot teach anybody anything; I can only make them think." To me, that is what Guy was doing.

As Lydia got older, he would give her distances and help her see the shot that would work with less chance for error.

"A lot of my coaching is for the student to take ownership over their own game. And getting that instilled in them early so they will have the mindset to be able to do the hard yards on the range and enjoy it. It's not a job, it's not a task because obviously the game of golf at times will beat you up and spit you out."

He taught and guided Lydia as well as all his students the importance of a pre-shot routine and visualization. "That is the time when I used my experience to help her see what I'm seeing – what I'm seeing in slopes, wind, hazards, trees and the like. I didn't want her to say here's where I got to go and ignore the other things around in her peripheral view. I did that often with Lydia when we played and it's a highly important step."

"A lot of my coaching is for the student to take ownership over their own game. And getting that instilled in them early so they will have the mindset to be able to do the hard yards on the range and enjoy it. It's not a job, it's not a task because obviously

the game of golf at times will beat you up and spit you out."

"That doesn't mean the student won't make mistakes. But when Lydia was a small child, and we played the course or later in tournaments I would help her 'see the shot' and she learned that quickly as other students do as well."

I asked Guy about swing thoughts.

"If she was correcting a fault, she might have a swing thought, but it was more important to keep calm and keep smiling."

Guy has seen wonderful things happen when he coaches children. "We often start coaching the kids. When the parents or siblings see them progressing and enjoying the game, they all want to get into it. And that leads the whole family and uncles and aunts into a playing golf lifestyle.

"Golf is a perfect sport to blend parents and family with their kids and they can play against each other fairly with handicaps.

"I tried to make it more enjoyable and more vibrant for Lydia. I had the IOMIC Company in Japan make special-colored grips for her clubs to better personalize what she was doing. She thought these were very cool."

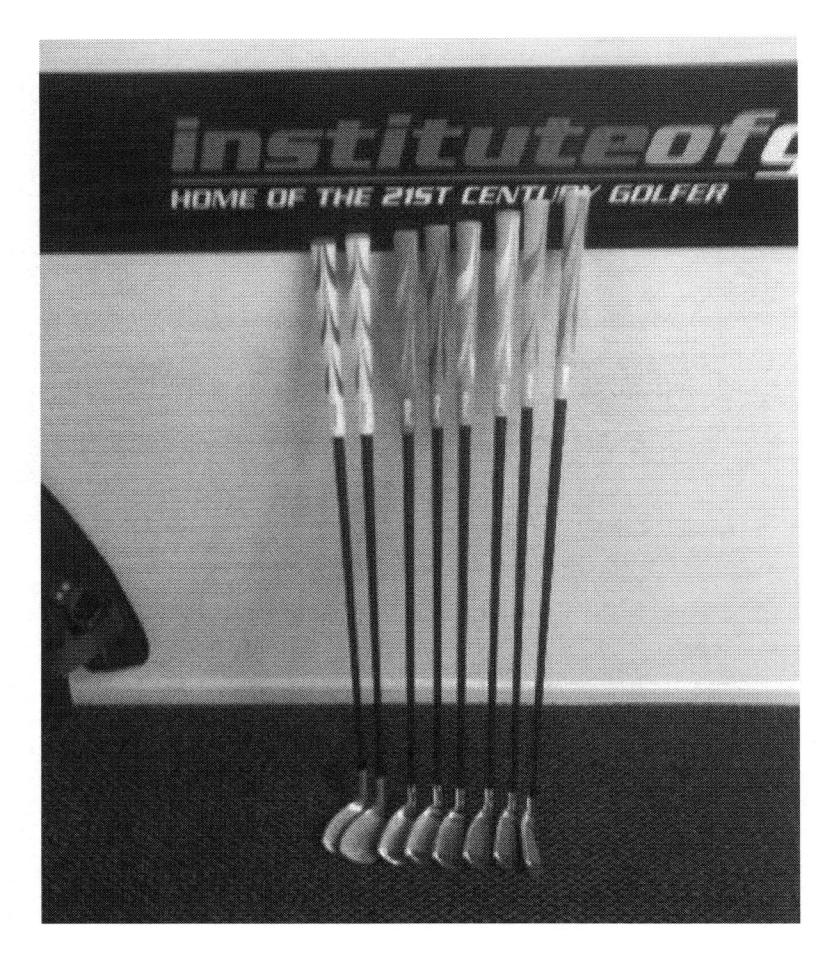

(Picture courtesy of Guy Wilson)

"I also had head covers made to personalize what she was doing."

Putting: The Yips & Positivity

"Around the clubhouse they tell you even God has to practice His putting. Even Nicklaus does."

-- Jim Murray

Practicing at Gulf Harbour Country Club (Picture courtesy of Guy Wilson)

Guy is coaching 14-year-old Lydia in this picture. Spine angle, connection, and face angle are important parts of putting.

2022 LPGA statistics show Lydia is putting well on the LPGA tour ranking 2nd (28.61 putts) on average putts per round. [14]

"Putting was one of the toughest parts to improve because making putts is where the rubber met the road in terms of score. I coached Lydia just to be aware of keeping her club face as square as she can during the first foot of its motion.

Did Lydia ever have problems?

"Yes. We did a lot around her grip back in the day because she got to a point where she would nearly start having the 'yips' over short putts."

Yips! What did you do?

"I got her to go left-hand low on short putts and right-hand low on long putts. I'm not sure, but I believe to this day she still goes left-hand low on short putts.

"Lydia does hit a lot of greens and that was amazing. She'd hit the fairway, hit the green, and have a 10-foot birdie putt, and so on. But she wouldn't hole a lot of birdie putts -- especially in big events.

"Both of us would get frustrated. It almost got to the point of being an Achilles heel since a lot of the other golfers we were playing with didn't have very many opportunities to make birdies. But it seemed that when they did, they would make it.

"Whereas Lydia might have 10 putts within 10 feet and make just one. That happened so often it tended to make her become negative about putting. So, we would try and find many ways of making putting enjoyable for her.

"I made recordings with positive affirmations for her and would email them to her to listen to at night. Things like 'You can make the putt' and many other affirmations."

Guy explained he sometimes uses tennis balls to practice putting. "When we were at the New Zealand Open in Christchurch at the Pegasus Golf Course, I would get her to putt with tennis balls. If she could hole a tennis ball into a golf hole it would make the hole seem huge to her when putting a golf ball. We did other things as well so putting wouldn't be such a challenge, but the object of it all is to avoid that moment you start thinking something is hard. Since if you get negative, golf really eats away at you."

Those are wise words in my opinion, as bad putting, or getting negative looking at a tough pin placement, and things like that can get you down fast. And sometimes it stays in a person especially when it's overemphasized, and if it's exaggerated, it perpetuates itself and can even breed more negativity. [15]

Guy's view is, "Negative energy attracts negative things. and the counter to that is that positive energy attracts positive things. I didn't want missing putts to be something that stayed with her. And that's why we changed the grip, we changed the color of the grip, the line on the ball, we even changed the ball marker – anything just to revitalize that relationship around putting.

"She would continue to use the same ball marker if a lot of putts were being made when that marker was used. Anything that produces a positive affirmation and calms her."

"We kept it all positive, and I knew it was just a matter of time before she would improve her play."

"Negative energy attracts negative things. and the counter to that is that positive energy attracts positive things."

Positives are a plus in golf, and sometimes positive superstitions work well. Some golfers make sure they keep their clubs in the same order in the bag every time. Others don't ever use ball washers before playing a shot over water. Some don't ever use a certain colored tee or a certain numbered golf ball. Most of us don't mention or talk about our score until the round is done.

Sound trivial? Tiger Woods wears red shirts on Sundays, Jack Nicklaus always had three coins in his pocket (he likes the number 3), Ernie Els gets rid of every ball he sinks for a birdie because he firmly believes there's only one birdie per ball, and many more famous players use superstitions to breed positive thoughts.

Negative attitudes and behavior generally lead to lower productivity, neglect, procrastination, and low morale. [16]

Guy and Lydia at Jack's Point GC (Picture courtesy of Guy Wilson)

Having Fun

"Fun is one of the most important (and underrated) ingredients in any successful venture. If you're not having fun, then it's probably time to call it quits and try something else."

-- Richard Branson

Due to budget constraints and his work at the Institute of Golf, Guy couldn't travel with Lydia to some of the tournaments he arranged for her to play in Australia. If he couldn't be there to help her, he created long-distance motivation by promising he would jump into a lake wearing his golf clothes if she won, and more.

Turned out Lydia won two Australian amateur events in a row and, yes, Guy jumped into a lake fully clothed twice!

Not stopping with just jumping in a lake, Guy promised if she won the Australian Ladies Masters at Royal Pines, he would dress up as a woman, with full make-up, and a golf bag over his shoulder, and jump into a lake. Lucky for Guy, she didn't win that one.

"I designed motivation by doing things if she succeeded. She never had to do anything negative if she lost. I always kept it positive by giving her a reward of a task I promised to do if she succeeded."

That's how bungy jumping came into the picture as mentioned at the beginning of this book at the Kawarau Gorge Suspension Bridge near Queenstown. [17]

Kawarau Gorge Suspension Bridge, Arrowtown NZ

Guy certainly did things if Lydia succeeded and one very special promise involved his engagement.

TVNZ's 1 NEWS is a major television station in New Zealand that has a program series called "Close Up". They featured Guy and Lydia in 2012.

The Interviewer for that feature was Ms. Abby Scott, a very attractive and successful television sports reporter. You can see the show on YouTube (see References endnote 18). [18] It's called, "Lydia Ko - Golfer - On Close Up in New Zealand with Coach Guy Wilson" [19]

Guy and Abby began dating after the filming of that show and continued dating for some time.

Lydia knew Abby and liked her. Guy promised Lydia he would propose to Abby after Lydia became the No. 1 ranked female golfer in the world.

Well, Lydia later became No. 1 in February 2017. By the way, that set another record for the youngest player ever, male or female, to be ranked No. 1 in professional golf. And that's younger than the greatest who have ever played the game, Bobby Jones, Arnie, Jack, Tiger, etc.

Guy proposed.

Lydia who was traveling at the time quickly gave her very warm congratulations to Guy and Abby via Twitter.

Giving More

"We make a living by what we get, but we make a life by what we give."

-- Winston Churchill

Guy helps all students as much as he can. That is just the nature of the man. Besides teaching Lydia how to play golf, he helped her and her parents in many other ways.

Lydia's parents were dedicated to her but neither played golf nor knew much about the intricacies of the golf world, golf tournaments, major U.S. university scholarships, raising funds, and more. Tina spoke English well, but Gil-Hong didn't speak English well.

Guy helped them with their daughter's school curriculum, raised funds so she could compete overseas, expanded her golf experience, attended long meetings with them and translators making sure they were all on the same page, and much more.

And he didn't charge them one cent for his time doing these additional things.

Schooling. Lydia's parents were not familiar with the New Zealand educational system. Guy was concerned about Lydia's education and wanted to make sure she was taking the right curriculum for college entrance as he knew major universities were going to be highly interested in her.

Lydia attended Pinehurst Elementary School in Albany and she is very bright. Guy knew she was a perfect candidate for almost any university. He arranged for Lydia's parents and himself to meet from time to time with her teachers to make sure Lydia was taking the right curriculum for college admission and hopefully a major university scholarship.

Lydia was excelling at golf and winning every match she had at Pupuke.

"We met with the school and regularly communicated with them to make sure she was taking the necessary courses that would also get her into a university… making sure they were providing her with a curriculum to qualify for admission to a university if say Stanford or another university offered her a scholarship program.

"Since she was getting to be an amazing player, we were also in constant communication with the school to ensure that she was getting as much time as she could playing golf and increasing her skill and developing her talents fully."

Expanding her experience. Guy wanted Lydia to gain more experience. "There was a lot more than coaching that I was doing to see Lydia prosper and I wanted her to get out and practice and play and learn as much as she could and for her to play other courses and practice at their driving ranges.

"The other courses were a bit reluctant at first since they were very protective of their facilities, and it wasn't easy for us to have Lydia practice at other courses.

"We persisted and got permission to use the driving ranges and golf courses at various golf clubs including a world-class course like Gulf Harbour Golf & Country Club designed by Robert Trent Jones, Jr."

At Gulf Harbour, there were other excellent junior golfers close to Lydia's age as well. Lydia remarked one of her favorite golf holes at Gulf Harbour was their signature hole, the long dogleg right and cliffside par 4 sixteenth hole. [20]

Translators. There were long discussions between Guy and Lydia's lovely parents. Guy wanted everyone involved to be kept up to date on Lydia's training and development.

"Long and full discussions were normal when dealing with an exceptional athlete. To be sure everyone was on the same page when I was coaching her, I asked her parents to have a translator at our meetings. They had Korean friends who were fluent in English who acted as translators at meetings which was very helpful to me so I could fully understand what Tina and especially Gil-Hong wanted for their little daughter."

Her parents were lovely, of course, and involved heavily with their daughter. Gil-Hong and Lydia spent a lot of time practicing with long practice sessions. Tina would do almost everything else.

Fundraising. Traveling to overseas tournaments is expensive.

"Her parents weren't rich, and I wasn't rich either. It was necessary and costly to travel overseas for Lydia to compete against others in the world and we needed to see how good she really was."

But Guy is a professional golf instructor who had no fundraising experience. And it's difficult to ask others for money, especially during tough economic times. But if you are determined to help someone, you find a way.

"I guess I was forced to do fundraising since I wanted to see Lydia progress and she was too young to do it herself of course. Her parents were Koreans with not a lot of golf expertise. I took on fundraising and learned there were a few foundations that support talented kids, and they were very happy to support her once I made them aware of her successes.

"Her parents and I wanted her to compete with people that would challenge her. The Ko's had a remarkable athlete for a daughter and not enough money to fund her traveling to overseas tournaments. It was tough."

Guy contacted Sir David Levene, a prominent and highly successful New Zealand businessman, and philanthropist.

"I met with David, and he knew Lydia from playing at Gulf Harbour Country Club and was interested in helping her.

"David became very valuable to Lydia's career and was hugely involved. He had his lawyers draw up a trust where people would be able to make donations for Lydia's continued development and travel overseas so she would be able to compete against the best in the world.

"At that time, Lydia was winning almost every local event, and there were only a few events in NZ that would challenge her."

Guy, Sir David, and others helped organize at Gulf Harbour the "Outward Bound Charity Golf Day" for Lydia to help her compete overseas and further her career. [21]

Many people thanked Sir David for his time helping Lydia and her family. David was a humble man who wasn't looking to draw attention to himself, but he nevertheless put his name and his own funds into the pot for Lydia.

"As it turned out, New Zealanders say his donations repaid everyone in New Zealand a thousand times over by raising the image of New Zealand around the world. [22]

Sir David Levene (1929 – 2021)

Lydia also received early financial support from the New Zealand Black & White Trust and other organizations.

Guy proceeded to have Lydia compete overseas in events that would challenge her like the American Junior Golf championships in the US and other events in Australia.

"The next three years were crucial for her. She wasn't getting enough experience in New Zealand as she was winning most every event she entered here, and she needed a more competitive scene to develop and grow her competitiveness. She improved by ridiculous amounts over the past three years, and I wanted to ensure that continued to happen."

Guy contacted other sources for funds and Golf New Zealand provided funds and others.

"There was always something to do to keep the machine running in the early days for Lydia. I had to deal with many obstacles and got through them."

Playing and Competing Overseas. Everyone knew 9-year-old Lydia was talented, but it remained to be seen how she would do against other golfers her age in the world.

Guy chose the 2007 Junior World Golf Championship in San Diego, a major tournament that attracted the top junior golfers from around the globe as a major test.

This event is held annually in San Diego usually at Torrey Pines Golf Course. Past junior girls' champions include Amy Alcott, Brandie Burton, Lorena Ochoa, and Jennifer Rosales. Past junior boy champions included Notah Begay III, Ernie Els, Phil Mickelson, Corey Pavin, Nick Price, Craig Stadler, David Toms, Jason Day, and Tiger Woods.

He discussed this tournament with Lydia's parents, and they agreed to give it a try.

Guy applied for a spot at this event. He stressed facts that New Zealand was a country not often represented in children's world golf competitions and Lydia's outstanding winning record in NZ.

His application for a spot for Lydia was accepted! This was going to be Lydia's first real trial. But then again, they were unsure how she would do.

"We were excited since Lydia was 9 years old. The field was very competitive and included the best junior golfers in the world including many skilled American children from the highly competitive US Junior Golf Program.

"And we didn't know how it would pan out. The tournament was 3 rounds of golf, and Lydia went into that tournament regularly shooting even par. San Diego had tough golf courses and Torrey Pines was one of the toughest. Lydia finished second at 3 under par - just 3 shots out of first place!

"Lydia, her family and I were all excited and very pleased with the second-place finish in her first major event. It gave us a real look at how Lydia was progressing compared to other golfers around the world." Lydia received a beautiful Second Place trophy competing in her first international golf tournament."

Guy then applied to Australian tournament committees by letting them know, "We have a girl ranked as the #5 amateur in the world and I gave them as much information as I could to get her a spot in these events."

Most responded by saying "She's a bit young but okay."

He traveled with her and Tina to tournaments in the Melbourne area, the Gold Coast, and other tournaments in Australia.

As time went by, Lydia began improving and getting accustomed to competitions. He arranged for her to compete in more Australian tournaments, and more NZ events.

She was doing well, and it was time to visit the U.S. again. "I arranged for a spot for Lydia in the 2009 Junior World Golf Championship in California and again, she won 2nd place.

Lydia competing in the 2009 World Junior Golf Championship at Torrey Pines Check out the colors on the grip and shaft (Picture courtesy of IOG).

As the great footballer, Pele, said, "Success is no accident. It is hard work, perseverance, learning, studying, sacrifice and most of all, love of what you are doing or learning to do."

Lydia held the trophy after winning 2nd place at the World Junior Golf Championship 2009 (Picture courtesy of IOG).

Covering all aspects – The Mental Game

"Golf is 90 percent mental, and the other 10 percent… is mental."

-- Jim Flick

Jim Flick made a good point!

Hall of Famer, Tommy Bolt said, "The mind messes up more shots than the body."

Guy like all excellent instructors wants students to learn all aspects of the game including the mental game.

In a previous chapter, I explained how Guy arranged for Lydia to meet with David Niethe a high-performance sports coach who worked with Lydia from the time she was 8 years old.

David also works with many other high-performing athletes such as World Champion Mixed Marshall Artist, Israel Adesanya, and many other world-class athletic champions.

I had heard of David and was interested in interviewing him. I wanted to learn how he produces the amazing results he achieves with the athletes he counsels.

By the way, David is also an athlete engaging in Rowing, Rugby, and the Highland Games. He's also competed in the New Zealand Strongest Man competition where he set new records. His passion for Golf has made him become one of the most highly sought-after golf performance coaches.

He's also worked with Company Directors, Managers, Business Owners, and Sales Managers helping them achieve success.

He's an educated man with certifications from the American Board of Neuro Linguistics and is a Master NLP Practitioner (ABNLP). He also is a Master Time Line Therapist (ABTL) and has a Master Hypnotherapist (ABH) certification.

David's favorite quote is – "Perception is projection", i.e., what you think is what you get!

I began by asking David about how he teaches his clients to stay in the "performance window" while competing.

He explained, "I think the mind is one of the most fascinating untapped human organs and there is so much unknown. We know more about the universe than we do the deep sea. And we know more about the deep sea than we do about consciousness. So, the brain is basically untapped. And I find that fascinating."

"It's called the performance window (a term David created), where we don't want to be excited, and we don't want to be passive either. A golfer needs to concentrate on the shot and be focused on the shot.

"And if a golfer executes a great shot that lands say 6 inches from the pin and the crowd goes crazy, the golfer needs to subtly say 'thank you', and not get overexcited. Likewise, if the golfer hits a terrible shot, the golfer should ideally not get overexcited.

"The 'performance window' is that place or mindset where a golfer takes control of what he or she focuses on. In the performance window we don't get passive, we don't get aggressive, we maintain an assertive mindset."

I thought that was very fascinating! In the zone... Dissociating oneself from the distracting aspects of the surroundings... I continued with my questions.

Q. "But what about a situation where you have a simple chip and chunk it and hit a terrible shot?"

"If you're confident out there and having fun, then you can perform in a way where even if you hit a bad shot, you can stay in that performance window."

I asked David if he uses hypnosis in training his clients.

"Occasionally. I use hypnosis to help visualize the relaxation process. The subconscious mind has no concept of reality and time."

David went on to explain that during the 1990s he competed in New Zealand's "World's Strongest Man" competitions and that is when he got interested in hypnosis.

"I didn't want to do steroids. So, I decided hypnosis instead of steroids. And I used the Neuro-Linguistics psychology of excellence.

"But what has happened in the last 20-30 years is that now it's starting to get quite scientific. It's removed from an individual process. Now highly competitive sportspersons would rather go to someone to work on the mental side of the game."

I was intrigued by David's direct manner and excellent mind.

Q. Tell me about the high-performance window.

"Here is what I teach athletes.

"Under any stressful situation, we have a natural response. People become one of these:

1. Aggressive

2. Assertive

3. Passive and internal

"In most cases, people either get aggressive or become internal and get passive.

"Being in an aggressive or passive state is not being in the performance window. The performance window is being in an assertive state, and there are three stages of assertiveness, and the ideal stage is calm.

"You don't make good decisions when you're angry or upset. The key to golf -- the challenge to golf isn't so much 'this screwed me'. The technical side of golf -- the challenge of golf is that it gives you time to think and to stay calm.

"You'll notice Lydia or other high-performance golfers are calm since they know to stay in the window and to stay in the window consistently.

"The second stage of being in an assertive state is happiness. When you're in a happy state it sets the right neurology, and you need the right neurology. I say to my clients, 'Stand up and put your hands together and look up to the ceiling, look way up, and put a smile on your face. And without changing get depressed.'

"Now to get depressed you must change your physiology. So, when you learn to consistently control your physiology by being in these two states, you then consistently become more consistent and that becomes habitual.

"The last stage of being assertive is Nietzsche's Superman Theory and that is having an undoubtable belief in oneself.

"You need absolute confidence because when you play golf, and you're in the performance window and you know you're going to put it right there. Your self-talk, your physiology, is in the performance window because you are being focused.

"Golfers have moments when they know they are superman or superwoman. You see them happy and calm. You don't see them getting down on themselves or angry.

"There are other key factors. Number one and what was beautiful is the fact that a high-performing athlete should be in love with the sport.

"Someone once said to me, 'What's the key to sport success? I say the key to success to a certain point was a question that I was constantly asked, 'Are we going further?'

"A successful golfer's success is an underlying success and quality of life. Performance is directly related to the quality of the questions you ask yourself.

"So, instead of saying why is this so hard, ask yourself a quality question such as, 'Can I just hit one more?'

"Now, that seems very simplistic but what you must appreciate is the next thing that supports it is, 'What's done in the dark will shine in the light' and you outwork everyone.

"When people ask me, I want to be a high performing golfer. I tell them, 'Okay I'm going to hold you to account for that.' Now, this doesn't guarantee anything, but it does improve probability. I ask them how long do you practice a day? They might say two hours or so. I tell them they should try tripling that and see if they get better results."

David isn't a counselor. Rather he teaches by dialogue between himself and his students to stimulate critical thinking like the Socratic method where the teacher poses thought-provoking questions engaging the student to ask questions.

I continued asking questions and his answers were very captivating in my view.

Q. Do you serve as a counselor to your clients?

"I'm not a counselor. I truly have a style where I hold people to account. It's not everyone's cup of tea. One of the first things I do with a client that comes in I'll ask them a question: Do you give me permission to be blunt and honest?

"If you want to be a high-performance athlete and I'll tell you that I don't think you have what it takes to perform in the high-performance area. That wouldn't be good in a counselor's role.

"What the key things are is teaching them through their self-awareness to auto-regulate their neurology and physiology and their perceptions.

"For me, it's about undoubtable belief in oneself. It's about being able to put their minds into the appropriate state to be effective.

Q. The performance window concept is intriguing. But how do you put your mind in the performance window and keep yourself there?

"When you have a good strong self-image as you golf to a certain point, it is then about recovery. In other words, you don't need to have to worry about the psychological when things are going well. But when things aren't going well you must find a way to put the best version of yourself in play to get the best possible score.

"If you are a pro you can't afford to drop shots. There is a lot of quality in golf today. So, it's about protecting the golfer's self-image and his or her understanding of what contributes to playing good golf.

"The key here is self-awareness. You don't make good decisions when you are upset or depressed or angry. Golf is about having the right mindset and excellent decision-making.

"I've worked with the New Zealand archery team and the New Zealand shooting team. Those sports are very similar to golf. In those sports, the brain tends to reach the last thing focused on.

"When we can get into an altered state, the peripheral shuts down and the brain focuses on the specific target, and this takes a whole new level of specificity into the pre-shot routine.

"Then it's about visual rehearsal with kinesthetic reinforcement. e.g., the practice swings. Then transition to target orientation.

"The brain likes targets. That is all about assuring the brain and then you make good decisions and assessments.

"Golf amateurs say, I do that, and I hit the shot, but I forgot about the elevation, or I forgot about the wind, as I went through the pre-shot protocols.

"Professionals are exceptionally good at assessment and have a very good pre-shot routine visually rehearsing the shot and going through the decision-making protocols, i.e., where they want the ball to stop -- last target orientation. Pre-shot routine is essential."

Q. David, you talked about being calm as one of the most important stages in being assertive when you are in the performance window. Would you please explain that more?

"Be brutality calm and focused. Because when you're calm it improves the probability of making good decisions. Golf to a certain extent is a puzzle. Where should I put the ball, etc., etc? So, to make good decisions you must be in that appropriate state.

"For a lot of athletes, golf is a fluctuation in physiology. I mean you probably have friends, and you can tell how well they are doing based on their physiology. For example, you'll see my clients on the course, and they remain calm.

"Golfers want consistency. What's the key to consistency? It is consistency in state of mind. Consistency in neurology and consistency in physiology set the foundation to make exceptionally good decisions to support the self-image and to build consistency of scoring."

Q. But what if you hit the perfect shot and a sudden and unpredictable gust of wind occurs and blows the ball into a water penalty area? I imagine that most golfers would exit the performance window, slam a club, etc. What do you teach when that happens?

"I'll show you. Again, it's about self-awareness. Things happen. I mean that's life, right? What happens is that naturally, you'll find people will fluctuate. They will get angry. Then they will get down on themselves.

"Some will get back in the window and some won't. The key thing is what you can appreciate through self-awareness.

"The first thing is to get agreement. Being angry or depressed doesn't contribute to being in a high-performance state or being the best, you can absolutely be and not fluctuating.

"However, we fluctuate. Now here is what I'm interested in. When things are going well, and you are in the high-performance window, ask yourself what you are like when you get into that state. So, as far as we know, when you're aggressive or passive, the neurology goes out the window. And as far as we know, it's different with each person as their mind interprets it as fight or flight or freeze.

"What we do know is that the neurology associated with those states is not ideal to make good decisions and not the ideal state we need to have to be in the high-performance window. It is ideal to be in the high-performance window. What we know is that when we get angry the brain reacts and releases hormones that are counterproductive to performance.

"But the one thing we need in golf is tempo and when the tempo goes bad, so does your golf. So, what I teach my clients is that everyone wants to be consistent. If you were consistently brilliant, you would take in the money, wouldn't you?

"So, what I'm interested in is how angry you get and what time passes for you to get back into the window. It's about self-awareness. So, once you recognize you are out of the window, do breathing."

Q. Breathing? What do you mean?

"Breathe in through the nose for 4 seconds. Hold for 5 sec and breathe out slowly through the mouth for 5 seconds or so. And then you will start feeling calm.

"This breathing approach is simplistic and repeatable. The difference between me and a psychologist is this. A car manual will help you understand the parts of a car, including brakes, carburetor, etc. I don't explain the parts of a car to my clients. I tell them how to drive it.

"And I do this for all sports, fencing, archery, swimming, mixed martial arts, boxers, golfers, rugby players, and more."

Q. What if the breathing doesn't work?

"It's not negotiable but it is also something to be continuously worked on. If you do the breathing effectively, it will serve you.

"It's about discipline, it's about training yourself to practice breathing. If you don't you have not taken responsibility.

"When I work with clients, I tell them if you start making excuses, like 'It doesn't work all the time.'

Then I ask them, 'Do you want to be the best? You need to continue the breathing to train the brain to put yourself in the appropriate performance window of best performance. There is no other way! There is no other method! It's about commitment to it! No excuses! Continue doing it to train the brain.'"

Q. Yes, I see. To keep yourself in the performance window you must discipline yourself to do the breathing. No excuses. Is that what you're saying?

"Yes. The secret is to be consistent doing that and it will become habitual an improve consistency. It is a combination of consistency in physiology and psychology that sets the foundation for performance."

Q. So if you continually practice breathing to keep yourself in the high-performance state, does it become habitual?

"You'll find that my clients don't have to breathe now. They have already trained the brain to return into the high-performance state. It becomes ingrained in their psyche. You won't have to think about being calm. You will be consistently calm if you discipline yourself to practice breathing."

Q. David, you teach many high-performing athletes. What is your advice about the mental game for an average or recreational golfer who wants to play better but doesn't have the time to practice? In other words, what do you tell a social golfer who just wants to get lower scores but has a day job, family duties, and many other things they must do every day?

"Anytime you recognize you're not in the state of the performance window. The first protocol is to breathe."

Q. What if you are an average golfer and you are playing with an annoying person that joins your group and you find it's affecting your play and enjoyment of the game?

"If the guy is annoying and an ass, I tell him in no uncertain terms to stop it or get lost! We teach people how to treat us. You say, 'You don't talk that way to me.'

"When you have a solid sense of self, when you have confidence and a strong self-image, then it's easy to be frank in communication. If you endure it, then you feel an obligation to be polite."

"We teach people how to treat us. When you have a solid sense of self, when you have confidence and a strong self-image, it's easy to be frank in the communication. If you endure it, then you feel an obligation to be polite."

Q. Well, this has been enlightening. I'm surprised I haven't heard more about you in the media, David.

"You don't tell people how good you are, let them tell you. I am someone you've never heard of. But you have heard of my clients. That's me doing my job. Do a good job, people will talk, and you will get referrals, which is the ripple effect.

"The other thing you got to appreciate about Guy is when Lydia came into the limelight, the focus was always on Lydia. Guy being Guy -- he was not one to say, 'Hang on! – look at me.' He was wonderfully comfortable with Lydia in the limelight.

"When you asked me to be interviewed by you I did so and had a sense of obligation out of respect for Guy as I think he definitely needs recognition.

"In New Zealand, we give all the attention to Lydia, and no one really thought of or appreciates fully the sacrifices, the work that Guy had done. Focusing on Lydia wasn't Lydia's doing. It was more about the media since they focus on the star.

"They forget that star was born from a great supportive team and obviously Guy is the key individual."

That reminded me of what I had read about true and genuine leaders such as Guy who believe the best way to find yourself is to lose yourself in the service of others. His leadership and dedication to coaching show he has a strong character and great integrity that not only fulfills his heart but also has a tremendous and lasting effect on the people he teaches.

David Niethe – (Picture courtesy of IOG)

Teaching Sportsmanship and Dealing with Competition

"Somewhere behind the athlete you've become and the hours of practice and the coaches who have pushed you is a little girl who fell in love with the game and never looked back ... play for her."

– Mia Hamm, former professional soccer player, and Olympic gold medalist

Teaching kids the value of good sportsmanship goes a long way in shaping their characters. It inspires and motivates them to give one hundred percent. Besides that, they learn how to play focused and fairly and learn to always play by the rules whether someone is watching or not. Being disciplined and honest is certainly an important value children can use in their entire life.

We all know competing in golf is different from competing in most sports. It's not like tennis where winning means you hit the ball back at your opponent as hard as you can beyond his control.

It's often been said that competition builds character and produces stronger determination, despite its stresses and pressures.

There was a recent study involving more than 11,000 children in the U.S. ages 9 -13 that found that children involved in team sports (golf team competitions are intense among universities) are less likely to have signs of anxiety, depression, withdrawal, or social problems. [23]

The researchers found children who compete in team sports have less difficulty socially because they learn to understand how others think. [24]

Organized competitions can promote a growth mindset (a growth mindset means those who believe their talents can be developed through hard work, good strategies, and input from others) plus stronger resilience. [25]

Golf is, of course, a complicated game where you are playing against a course using clubs, trying to hit a little 1.620 oz. ball, while focusing, controlling your mind, relaxing your physique, and relying on your coordination to hit the shot you want to hit.

So, how does a coach handle young, growing, and active children who still may have a lot to learn about discipline? And how does a coach teach students to deal with competition and disappointing defeat?

Cecilia Cho and Lydia first met playing inter-provincial (regional) golf competitions. Lydia was playing for the North Harbour region and Cecilia was playing for the Auckland region.

Guy recalled, "Their parents got to know each other realizing they had a lot in common with both families being Korean and having a child interested in golf. At that time, Cecilia was better than Lydia, but Cecilia was one or two years older."

Even though their families lived in the Auckland area, geography, and traffic made it difficult to become close friends. "Cecilia was older and lived quite a distance from Lydia. Because of the regional distances involved and Lydia being younger, it was difficult for Lydia and Cecilia to become close friends although they both enjoyed playing golf."

In March 2011, Cecilia Cho became the World's No. 1 amateur in World Amateur Golf Rankings. She lived with her family in the Auckland area.

Cecilia was an impressive golfer with 16 wins in New Zealand along with many other awards.

Newspapers in New Zealand reported that Cecilia and Lydia were "rivals" since Lydia was also winning many events and ranked in the top 3 in World Amateur Rankings.

As far as Guy knew there wasn't any strong "rivalry" so to speak. He treated Cecilia as more of a benchmark. "After Cecelia was ranked the No. 1 amateur, I started looking into the rankings and other things. Cecilia's performances were a measure for us. Lydia and I would share thoughts on how we were doing compared to Cecilia in tournaments."

Everyone knows there are good and bad things when children compete. The good things are competition teaches social skills, learning to control emotions, being more resilient, and more good things.

Some, however, feel children competing against each other may not be healthy since it may,

- Lead to injuries to children who might be pushing their developing bodies too far.

- Lead to dropping out.

- Start to deflate their own self-worth.

- Be disappointing.

- Lower confidence.

- Cause unnecessary stress, and other negatives.

The study of children competing in teams which I cited earlier seems to say healthy competition is good since it gives children the opportunity to strive to do the best they can, and the opportunity to learn good sportsmanship – things we all need in any avenue we choose in life.

Whether you feel competition is good or bad is strictly your decision for your child.

Golf competitions have existed since the sport began hundreds of years ago. Guy showed Lydia how to treat the competition with a positive attitude.

"If Lydia lost to Cecilia, we viewed it as Cecilia was older and stronger, had more distance, and had been playing golf longer.

We treated Cecilia's scores and tournament results as a measure for younger Lydia.

"In the tournaments we entered, we would see how Cecilia did since she was the World's Number 1 ranked amateur. We would simply compare how we did with how well Cecilia did."

Guy told me about a match between Lydia (playing provincial golf for the North Harbour Team) and Cecilia (playing for Auckland Team) that determined the winner of the New Zealand Golf Provincial Championship.

In the final match, Lydia was on the 18th green, and Cecilia had already holed out on the 18th with a par.

Lydia had only about a 20-foot birdie putt to win the final match against Cecilia.

Even if Lydia two-putted she would halve the match and a half would result in a victory for North Harbour Team and the Championship for the team!

So, a simple two-putt would result in a Championship win for the North Harbour Team.

However, if Lydia 3-putted that would result in a loss in her match against Cecilia, and a loss would result in the Auckland Provincial Team winning the Championship.

"I couldn't remember Lydia ever 3 putting on a fairly straight putt from that distance. She knew she only needed a two putt for a North Harbour Championship win, but she unbelievably three-putted."

I asked Guy how he handled that.

"I didn't say one word about it."

Sometimes not saying anything is the best answer. Guy stood by Lydia showing her his support.

Both Guy and Lydia silently knew there would be another day.

"I told Lydia, and we always had the same philosophy that the past is the past and to keep looking forward. There's nothing you can do about another competitor and the only thing you can control is your own game."

And sure enough, the competition between Cecilia and Lydia came to a head across the ditch (i.e., the Tasman Sea) in the 2011 Australian National Amateur Stroke Play Championship. Lydia again was playing Cecilia in the final match and after 18 holes it was all square. And that resulted in a sudden-death playoff for the Championship.

Lydia won it on the second playoff hole.

Not stopping there, Lydia beat Cecilia again in the New Zealand Stroke Play Championship. Cecilia came in second.

The next event was the New Zealand Match Play Championship and Cecilia had won it for the past two years.

Lydia and Cecilia again were playing in the final match at Russley Golf Course in Christchurch.

Lydia ended that match early being 4 up with 3 to play!

Guy recalled, "Everyone celebrated and that was the week of Lydia's birthday as well!"

After that event, Lydia was ranked the No. 1 amateur in World Amateur Rankings, and that three-putt on the 18th in the NZ Provincial Match was long forgotten. And Lydia remained the No. 1 amateur for the next 2 ½ years.

Guy was of course pleased with that win, but again, the past is the past and he always kept looking ahead for more events to challenge Lydia for her to gain more experience.

Moving from Pupuke Golf Club to the Institute of Golf

"To improve is to change; to be perfect is to change often."

-- Winston Churchill

After over 10 years at Pupuke Golf Club, Guy moved his coaching a short distance away. "I moved from Pupuke Golf Club to nearby Albany and joined Craig Dixon."

"Did Lydia follow you?" I asked.

"Lydia followed and I continued her instruction at IOG. It's an extensive and world-class golf center, with Physio Training facilities there." [26]

Everyone at the Institute of Golf strives and knows how to get the best out of people and enable more players to achieve their best game. They believe that with "enjoyment comes achievement, and with that comes a game that is healthy and growing."

"Also, at IOG I now had the opportunity to consult with the other coaches and we were the first high-performance golf coaching facility in New Zealand. So, the response was tremendous.

"I liked the way the coaches at IOG discussed students together and brainstorm the best way to benefit the students.

"Every elite golfer in New Zealand wanted to use IOG so we mainly coached low-handicap golfers and professional players at that point.

"The coaches at IOG discussed students together and brainstorm the best way to benefit the student."

"At IOG, we added Physio Training as part of our golf improvement program and established a gym there with professional physiotherapists.

"Tiger was one of the first professional golfers to emphasize the importance of physio training and the athletics of golf. But at that time there were no programs or recipes for Junior golfers to train their bodies. I wanted to make sure I wasn't leaving any stone unturned.

"She would hit hundreds of balls a day so it is important for Lydia to have a good tempo and an efficient, rhythmic, and well-balanced swing that would not cause damage to her body. The physio experts would choose what was more ideal in her movements and patterns and longevity to make sure she would not suffer injury if she used that swing over long periods.

"I would discuss this a lot with them. The swing we had when were at Pupuke through her younger years changed dramatically when she came to IOG. The physiotherapy team provided input and suggestions about having Lydia in the correct body position when she is hitting hundreds of balls a day.

"A lot of the golf swings can be detrimental to a person's body and Lydia was young and still growing and the physios had good advice to make sure the spine would work well in this position, and the arms would work well in this position, and I combined those to produce a healthy swing that would last and not cause injury. It was also important to make sure rhythm and tempo were working well.

"I liked to use technical aids at IOG such as FlightScope, Trackman and K-Vest. K-Vest helps a coach and the student make sure the right movements are being made with the right muscles."

Guy continued coaching Lydia at IOG and other students as well. Golf coaching, like any other sport requires continuing education on many new concepts and theories about the golf swing, golf fitness, and other aspects of golf that evolve.

Guy, like the many students he coaches, believes in always learning new things especially, using the latest state-of-the-art technology. "I used Putt-Lab and other technical aids as well."

Technical aids provide ready information for coaches to help students improve faster and pinpoint areas that need improvement.

Guy uses a new program called, "Draw More Circles" a shot data program" that uses Artificial Intelligence (AI) to analyze data and shows the coach and student exactly what areas of the student's game are doing well and what areas need more improvement.

It makes practicing more efficient, and improvement comes faster. More on this later in the book.

Developing More

*"Success is a journey, not a destination. The doing is often
more important than the outcome."*

-- Arthur Ashe

In 2010, Guy arranged for Lydia to play in more major
tournaments getting her spots on the Women's World Amateur
Team where she tied for 31st competing against the best adult
women amateurs in the world.

Lydia also played in the New Zealand 3-person team for the
Queen Sirikit Cup which is officially known as the Asia-Pacific
Amateur Ladies Golf Team Championship. This is a world
event, but it was played in New Zealand that year and the New
Zealand Team won second place playing against the other
teams from many countries in the Asia-Pacific.

There has always been a lot of high performing up and coming
golfers in the world. It is impossible (unless you have a genuine
crystal ball) to determine or predict for sure who among them
is going to be above all the rest one day.

I asked Guy if there was ever a time when he first realized he
was molding someone who would be very special.

For example, did Lydia as a 10 or 11-year-old ever hole out from different positions 10 thirty-foot putts in a row or pitch 9 out of 10 balls from 50 meters out to three feet from the pin?

"You really don't know if a student is going to be a great golfer at practice sessions. Practice is only one aspect in golf. The real sign of being great is how the student can perform against the high performing golfers in tournament play," he explained.

"Golf is a journey and there isn't a time when you have an awakening of greatness. Perhaps the first time I had a strong realization that Lydia was going to be something very special was at the New Zealand Women's Open at the Pegasus Golf Course in Christchurch in 2010.

"That tournament was just made part of and co-sanctioned by the European Ladies Golf Tour. Some of the best women professional golfers in the world were competing against each other. I arranged for a spot for Lydia when she was only 12 years old, and I caddied for her.

"The 2010 tournament was won by World Golf Hall of Fame member Laura Davies. Lydia was hitting the ball so well and had so many great birdie opportunities. Lydia was not making many of the birdie opportunities and still managed to finished as the lead Kiwi and the lead amateur finishing only 8 shots behind Laura Davies in her first professional event.

"The putting throughout that tournament made me take a step back and reflect on her lessons and hard work. I strongly realized all of that was paying off for her well. But we still had a lot to work on and golf is a journey that takes time."

Through a highly influential New Zealander whom Guy coached, it was arranged for Guy, Lydia and her mother Tina to be hosted by Larry O'Neill, the former golf coach at Stanford University in California.

"Larry played with us, and he introduced us to local golf pros all increasing her confidence and experience."

Larry not only hosted them but also arranged for them to play at the world-renowned Cypress Point Golf Club in Pebble Beach, California as well as the Stanford Golf Course where Tiger honed his game.

"When we played at Cypress Point, Lydia was leading through something like 14 holes, I'm not exactly sure. She wasn't playing too well then, I ran out of balls, and we laughed and laughed. She wound up beating me by 5 strokes and shot 1 over par on that course."

After that visit, Larry O'Neill wrote this letter to Guy.

Hi Guy,

I want to congratulate you on the great foundation you built in Lydia Ko. Anything you build you have to keep in mind how long it is going to last. Over the years you can make small changes, but a well-built foundation will last a lifetime.

I have been teaching golf for over 50 years and I see she has made a few changes, but the solid foundation is still there. Her grip looks good and on her regular swing, she gets the club in

93

a good position on top. I love the way she uses her legs to get over to her left side and a good high finish.

Some of those basic fundamentals were tough for her at a very young age. I hope her family thanked you along the way.

Well, my Kiwi friend this old Irish Yank wanted to tell you how I feel.

All the best,

Larry

In 2011, Guy arranged for her to play in the Australian Women's Strokeplay Championship, and she won that!

Lydia with the Australian Amateur Strokeplay Trophy (Picture courtesy of IOG)

Continuing, Guy arranged for her to play in many more events like the Australian Women's Amateur where she made the Quarterfinals, the Ladies British Amateur where she finished 32nd and she was a medalist in the U.S. Women's World Amateur Championship.

Guy had eyes on the prestigious 2011 U.S. Women's Amateur Championship. He was able to arrange for her to play in the required qualifying round which took place 3 weeks before the US Women's Open.

It would be costly to fly to the qualifying tournament, fly back to NZ, and fly back again for the US Women's Amateur Championship at The Rhode Island Country Club. So, they decided to make it a month-long trip to the U.S.

Lydia was successful at the qualifying event and finished a co-medalist in the US Women's Amateur, although she fell in the second round of Match Play.

The next year 2012 turned out to be an incredible year for Guy and Lydia. The solid foundation that Guy had given her over the past 11 years truly began to blossom.

On 29 January 2012, Lydia became the youngest person ever to win a professional golf tour event by winning the Bing Lee/Samsung Women's NSW Open on the Australian LPGA Tour. She was 14 at the time. The year before that she came in second. [27]

Lydia at the NSW Open (Picture courtesy of Guy Wilson)

Lydia at the NSW Open (Picture courtesy of Guy Wilson)

In 2012, Lydia also won the US Women's Amateur, finished tied for 17th at the Women's British Open, tied for 39th at the US Women's Open, finished 2nd at the Queen Sirikit Cup, and won the Australian Women's Amateur.

Later, at the age of 15 years and four months, Lydia, playing as an amateur, became the youngest-ever winner of an LPGA Tour event, winning with a score of 275 (−13) at the CN Canadian Women's Open. [28] That broke the record set by Lexi Thompson at 16 years about a year earlier. [29]

Lydia's win made her the first amateur in over 43 years to win the CN Canadian Women's Open. [30]

Everyone knows an amateur doesn't get professional prize money. LPGA 1st place prize money is serious. The winner's share of the 2012 CN Canadian Women's Open is $300,000. Lydia didn't get a penny of that. That $300k went to runner-up Inbee Park who was in second place three strokes back. [31]

The next year, Lydia successfully defended her win at the 2013 CN Canadian Open, shooting 265 (−15) for a five-stroke victory over Karine Icher at the Royal Mayfair Club in Edmonton. But, again, she did not see a penny of that. The $300,000 winner's share went to Icher. [32]

The Guy Wilson and Lydia Ko team were winning against the best women players in the world. Should she turn pro?

Turning Pro at 16 – A child applying for LPGA membership. There were advantages to keeping amateur status as the major tournaments had spaces reserved for top amateurs. Turning pro too early might even make it harder to get a spot in a major.

Guy had discussions with Lydia's good parents about whether Lydia should get a scholarship to a major university and keep her amateur status or whether she should turn pro. At that time, Lydia's parents weren't rich, and money was tight. Just the expenses involved in playing on a professional golf tour were over $100,000 a year.

LPGA rules say you must be an adult to join the LPGA. The minimum age for eligibility to join is 18 years old. Lydia was only 16 years old. It was rare for anyone under 18 years old to turn pro.

So, end of story, right? But there is an old saying, "If others haven't laughed at your dreams, you're not dreaming big enough so keep pushing forward."

"I always wanted to keep her ahead of the curve," Guy said. "Lydia had already won two LPGA Tour events – the 2012 Canadian Open and the 2013 Canadian Open. So, why not apply early?"

As Dr. Suess wrote, "Why fit in when you were born to stand out?" So, with Lydia's parents' approval, Guy did the early application paperwork and arranged for Lydia to apply for an LPGA membership.

"I always wanted to keep her ahead of the curve. Lydia had already won two LPGA Tour events – the 2012 Canadian Open and the 2013 Canadian Open. So, why not apply early?"

He also wrote this letter of recommendation on her behalf (I think you can tell a lot about the kind of person Guy truly is when your read this letter).

4th October 2013,

Re: Lydia Ko LPGA Recommendation

To whom it may concern,

I would like to submit my recommendation for Lydia Ko to be admitted to the LPGA before she is officially eligible by age.

I have known Lydia since she was five years old and have coached her ever since. In those 11 years, I have seen Lydia go from strength to strength both on and off the golf course.

Lydia has shown not only her team but also the world that she has the skills and game to play alongside the world's best. Her technique and ability to tactically work her way around a golf course in the toughest of environments are among the best and

I believe she is going to be at the top of the women's game for years to come.

She is mature beyond her 16 years and is growing more and more comfortable around older players with every start she gets. Her maturity is constantly developing, and this will only grow the more time she spends on the tour. Although she is 16, she has been competing against professional golfers for over four years, since she was just 12 years old. As her profile has risen it's becoming increasingly hard for her to separate her on and off-course life, but she takes it in her stride and attempts to manage that the best she can. Her sunny disposition allows her to adapt to any situation and I have no doubt she'd thrive on the LPGA.

Lydia's mother manages a lot of the things off the course and is an integral part of her life. They are a great team and Tina allows Lydia to focus her attention on what she needs to do on the course without other distractions. I'm sure over the next few years Lydia will become more and more self-sufficient but I think she has a great support structure around her in the meantime. Lydia has spent the past 8???? Months away from home and practically on tour already and she has well and truly flourished. Joining the LPGA is a step that she is completely ready for and will adapt to easily.

Even when she was young Lydia was never far from the media spotlight and there had always been someone wanting her time. Lydia knows how important it is to give the media what she can so that her followers, fans, and the golfing community can be told of her movements. Given Lydia's rise over the past few years, more and more interviews have been requested and she has managed them fantastically. She is known by the media as a candid, funny, open, and engaging athlete to interview, and while she now has less time to offer, she always endeavors to do what she can. Her media presence has won the hearts of many Kiwis and others in the golfing world, and she is a fantastic role model for the sport. Someone who genuinely enjoys what she does and has worked hard to get there.

For a long time now, we have been purposely injecting Lydia into fields filled with players beyond her years. To date, she has not faltered. Her first professional event was the New Zealand Women's Open at age 12 where she finished 7th. No small achievement. Since then, she's gone on to win four professional titles, including two LPGA events, and came close to claiming a major, again never faltering.

Lydia's team has consciously made a decision not to rush any petition to the LPGA, but I have no doubt that now is the right time for Lydia to be admitted. She has the skills, the support structure, and the maturity to take on the next challenge, not to mention the results to back it up.

I would not hesitate in recommending her and given the amount of time we have spent together I feel that I have one of the best understandings of her on and off the course. If you would like to discuss this or anything else with me further, please don't hesitate to contact me on my personal numbers.

Yours sincerely,

Guy Wilson

Director of Instruction

INSTITUTE OF GOLF LTD.

Success! Just 25 days later Reuters News Agency reported that 16-year-old Lydia Ko has been granted full membership to the LPGA Tour beginning at the start of the 2014 season. The LPGA waived the 18-year-old age requirement for membership.

Commissioner Mike Whan was reported as saying, "After reviewing Lydia's petition, I have granted her LPGA Tour membership beginning at the start of the 2014 season." He also remarked it wasn't often they welcome a rookie who has back-to-back wins as an LPGA Tour champion. [33]

Lydia said it had been a dream goal to play in the LPGA against the world's best players and wanted to inspire other girls to take up the game and go for it as she did. [34]

Two months after turning professional, Lydia won her first event at the Swinging Skirts World Ladies Masters on the Korean Ladies Professional Golf Association Tour (KLPGA).

In the 2014 season, she played in 12 events, made 12 cuts, and had one victory, and five Top-Ten finishes.

Off to Orlando.

"Oh the places you'll go!

There is fun to be done!

There are points to be scored.

There are games to be won.

And the magical things you can do with that ball

will make you the winning-est winner of all."

> *— Dr. Seuss, "Oh, The Places You'll Go!"*

16-year-old Lydia and her parents moved to Orlando at the end of 2013 to begin her professional career managed by IMG a well-known U.S. global sports, events, and talent management company.

Guy said, "Lydia is a person who is heavily dependent on her team, and her parents felt they needed to find a team closer to where she was going to be."

Lydia told TVNZ's 1 NEWS, "It's obviously sad to stop with Guy. He's been a great coach and a great friend as well. But it's just important to know that we still are good friends." [35]

USA Today reported, "Ko has won five professional tournaments — four as an amateur — while coached by Wilson, who said it had "been an honor to help develop Lydia. When I first met her the golf clubs were taller than she was and she didn't know the first thing about a driver or a putter, but now she has one of the most envied swings in the women's golf world," [36]

Guy led Lydia to the world stage of Women's golf, and it all began eleven years ago in 2002 when Tina brought her little daughter into his pro shop.

"We've spent a lot of time together over the past decade and during that time I've become very close to Lydia and her family."

Guy certainly was a remarkable and genuine coach while not only helping a little girl develop exceptional golf skills but also a lasting positive attitude filled with the enjoyment of a game that sometimes can be devastating and mind-boggling.

Institute of Golf (IOG)

"We work with golfers of any age, from beginner to intermediate, who seek focus, direction and personalized attention on their game. The methods we use include one-on-one coaching, group lessons and our junior development program."

-- Institute of Golf

I was curious to learn more about the Institute of Golf and learned they will help anyone, from children to professionals who seriously want to improve their game.

They have three locations in the North Island of New Zealand in Albany, Takapuna, and Ellerslie.

If you learn golf as a child, you will be miles ahead of others when they discover the game years later. Having an edge over your peers while you're in your teens or twenties builds your confidence and you'll get admiration from your peers.

LPGA Hall of Famer Kathy Whitworth said, "Golf is a game of misses, and the winners are those who have the best misses."

I asked Guy about mishitting the ball. Many often miss hitting the ball with the center of the clubface. To determine exactly where any golfer is hitting the ball on the clubface check out

Guy's Facebook video is referenced in the back of the book in the References section (see 38) and the link. [37] Foot spray is all that's needed! The video has a simple technique that shows where you are hitting the ball on the clubface (heel, toe, top, bottom, or center). [38]

For mishits, the fastest way to correct them is technology. I asked Guy more about the coaches and technology available at IOG.

"At IOG, all our coaches use technology so students can understand where their weaknesses are throughout the golf swing versus just seeing the ball go off into the bush and saying, 'I'm useless at this.'

"Our coaches want the golfer to understand many facets of golf using state of the art technology. And they make it an enjoyable journey for every student as that is our goal -- to make sure the student is enjoying the time spent with the coaches and can understand the information easily."

NZPGA coach Grant Stockman speaks highly of IOG, "During my time working at the Institute of Golf, I was really impressed with how they run and go about their business from both an employee's perspective and the quality of the overall experience from the customer's point of view.

"The coaches have access to the best technology such as Trackman and IOG's latest addition of 'Data tracking software' which tracks every aspect of the student's game. This is an incredible new way to help both the client and the coach understand the finer and very factual details of what is really happening in a student's game.

"Having this information at your fingertips enhances the coach's ability to deal with student's strengths and weaknesses.

"A coach who is looking for an opportunity to grow and improve as a golf coach, should consider applying to the Institute of Golf. To anyone considering a role with IOG, I can assure you that you will be immersed in a great team of coaches and supported strongly by the company in all aspects of your role. I highly recommend taking the opportunity if it is available."

Technology brings people together so they can share information more effectively.

Here is a list of some of the technology they use.

The SAM Putt Lab. This is a unique high-tech system that measures and analyzes all movement details of putting and chipping. In practice mode, the short game can be improved to high levels.

Golfweek - USA Today Sports did an informative article on the SAM Putt Lab saying, "Christian Marquardt, managing director for Science and Motion and one of the device's inventors, said golf instructors Hank Haney and Dave Pelz were among the first to grasp SAM PuttLab's potential."

K Vest places sensors on the player using a vest, belt, and glove. The player makes swings, and the K-VEST software captures the swings so the coach can better assess and improve the swing.

It helps the coach and the player to build the basic movement patterns, strength, speed, balance, and flexibility that support the swing.

TrackMan is a well-known and popular radar system to track and records the 3D characteristics of a golf ball in motion. It measures aspects of the club movement, the trajectory of the ball, and its landing. It is equipped with a video camera so coaches and the students can watch themselves while looking at information about their swing. It's used by hundreds of golfers competing at the highest level. [39]

CoachNow is a digital training and communication platform for coaches, teachers, and trainers used internationally to maximize their efficiency and impact. It was created for coaches who are passionate about coaching smarter, who want to manage their time better and to inspire, motivate and change lives on and off the playing field. This platform enables better communication, elevated learning, and empowerment to coaches at any level. [40]

Draw More Circles program is a shot data program developed over the years and shows what areas the student needs to practice. It makes practice sessions more efficient and lower scores quickly. In other words, "Why hit 1,000 balls when the data shows you need to focus on chipping."

Circles helps a student understand and optimize practice time and uses Artificial Intelligence. Craig Dixon, co-Director at IOG, founded the Draw More Circles program so IOG students or anyone can use the kinds of tools the pros do without a hefty price tag.

Circles began with Craig Dixon who used it when he was involved in coaching the Chinese Women's Olympic team.

There is more in this book on this new technology later in the book. Here is one testimonial about "Circles" from Richard Woodhouse, a two-time Australian PGA Coach of the Year,

"I'm blown away by what Circles gives me insight into. The possibilities of this software and applicable training ideas are endless."

⚬━⚬⚬⚬⚬━⚬

IOG is also recognized by NZ Golf for PGA trainees who want to do their PGA traineeship at IOG.

Guy explained there is a camaraderie among the coaches at IOG. "The coaches here at IOG are not competitive with their fellow coaches since they are there for the players who want to be coached.

"We all evaluate and recommend a course of coaching action. We don't want to coach people just for the sake of coaching. Everyone at IOG makes sure the coaching time is used wisely so every student can progress to their goal."

Many new students want Guy as a coach, and he will schedule them if he can. But he explained that he will be the first to tell them, "There's no need to pay my coaching rates as there are high quality coaches here who can be effective for your child who teach at a high level. And with every student, we all discuss students together, and I can step in any time when help is needed."

"We all evaluate and recommend a course of coaching action. We don't want to coach people just for the sake of coaching. Everyone at IOG makes sure the coaching time is used wisely so every student can progress to their goal."

Often team at IOG evaluates and brainstorms students when he or she first comes into the IOG facilities and recommends a course of coaching action for the student if they have lofty goals.

A student may have two or several coaches. They want each student at IOG to use their time wisely.

Guy said, "All coaches are encouraged to ask the opinions of other coaches. Such as, 'I'm a bit stumped on this student. What's your input?'

"They work alongside each other and there is good synergy among the coaches as well as the students as they practice and play golf.

"At IOG, we try to ensure that everyone has a really good experience and loves their time with the coaching. We want all students to want to come back and do it again.

"We teach all golfers, junior golfers, junior golfers with professional aspirations, low handicap to high handicap players, older golfers, businessmen and women who have the time and want to improve their golf for business and personal reasons."

I was impressed with their facilities. I discovered they don't advertise as most of the business comes from word of mouth.

I asked Guy about coaching older golfers over 50 who aren't as flexible as younger golfers.

"If I or any coach here thinks any difficulty is more of a physical limitation then we recommend consulting with our physiotherapy department to assess them and determine what's possible and what's not possible swing-wise. They usually get treatment, or an exercise program to improve better parts of the body to enable them to play better as a golfer rather than fight physical limitations.

"After going through a physio program, we can take another look to see if it is really a physical limitation or a technical problem that we can correct. In other words, if it's physical the physiotherapists work to improve it. If it's technical then the coaches improve and work on it to get positive results."

Besides their three locations in the North Island, the coaches and students play and practice at other golf courses around New Zealand.

IOG has an excellent reputation overseas and foreign students visit to receive golf instruction. VIP businessmen come to IOG as well and hire IOG staff to go with them for instruction to various premier golf courses in New Zealand such as Millbrook, Kauri Cliffs, Cape Kidnappers, and more.

These clients not only receive excellent instruction but also enjoy some of the most beautiful courses in the world.

In other words, if it's physical the physiotherapists work to improve it. If it's

technical then the coaches improve and work on it to get positive results. "

Sections of IOG practice ranges are child-orientated with different colored pins and flags and more features. "We try to get their imagination running wild and not have them feel like they're on the back foot – since they are trying to play an adults game and be successful at young age," Guy said.

"We do competitions around the areas in our IOG center for children. It ranges from having little competitions during practice times, going to a golf course together, or attending tournaments and events to support other IOG students who may be playing in the tournament.

"I enjoy watching IOG students compete in tournaments, and we have our team around them, so they don't feel like they're out there by themselves. And that's what golf is – you're out there by yourself and it's great to have a team of coaches and players showing support and we don't charge for that time.

"We go there to support our students playing and review their data and that makes later coaching more effective. If for some reason, we can't watch all of them, we review their data and we can determine quickly where they need help to get better results in the next tournament."

I was surprised at the attention and care they give students. Most club pros at golf courses are extremely busy with a pro shop and club members to look after as well as their personal matters, and more all making demands on a club pro's attention and time.

"When Craig and I finished our PGA training, we did our time in the pro shop, managing club events and club members and the like. We enjoyed it but it wasn't our motivator.

"What we truly enjoy is coaching our students, introducing children to the game, teaching and guiding junior golfers as well as high-performing golfers. We simply enjoy helping anyone who wants to use our coaching and facilities at IOG centers."

For young children he uses games. "We will have closest to the pin, putting competitions, 'Lord of the rings', approach shot challenges, bunker games, team games, and using our technology to find a winner in most situations!"

Lord of the rings? I hadn't heard of that one.

"It's a game I created for children in a group lesson. For example, I place six flat vinyl rings each having a three-foot radius around 6 pin positions on our large practice green.

"Then there are six different chipping positions to chip from on the grass around the green say at 6 o'clock, 8 o'clock, 10 o'clock, 12 o'clock, 2 o'clock, and 4 o'clock.

"The children line up at the starting 6 o'clock position and take turns to see who can chip 4 consecutive balls inside the ring around the first cup. If they can chip 4 consecutive balls and have the balls stay inside the three-foot ring (it can easily roll through the ring since the ring is flat) the student can proceed to the next or 8 o'clock chipping position. If they don't do 4 consecutive balls inside the ring, then they must go to the back of the line and try again at the starting 6 o'clock position.

"If they chip 4 consecutive balls inside the ring, they can go on to the next or 8 o'clock position and see if they can chip 4 consecutive balls from the 8 o'clock position, and so on until they complete the circle around the practice green.

"The fun part is let's say a student makes it to the 12' o'clock position or even all the way to the 4 o'clock position chipping 4 balls consecutively inside the ring then misses chipping 4 consecutive balls inside the ring, the student must go all the way back and start all over at the 6 o'clock position.

"I also make variations to this game to keep it all entertaining for them."

That sounded like a lot of fun to me, and I plan on trying that out with my golf buddies instead of chipping ball after ball after ball.

The IOG center in Albany was certainly busy. I asked Guy to tell me more about IOG.

Guy explained, "We teach everyone. There are young and old golfers, children, junior golfers, junior golfers with professional aspirations, businessmen and women who have the time and want to improve their golf for business and personal reasons, and professional golfers... and complete beginners that want to give golf a go."

But what about the average golfer? The purely social golfer or over 50-year-old golfers. Do they use the new Circles program?

"Many adult golfers are getting back into the game after playing the game at a younger age or starting the game fresh. Their kids have grown up, and they now have more free time to enjoy the things they like to do or would like to do.

"All the coaches are familiar and understand the Circles platform. Anyone can use it. It's efficient and effective to target the areas they need to practice for better scoring. And that is the quickest way to get strokes off your game."

That made sense to me.

Guy said, "Often players tell the coaches what they FEEL they need work on but without data to support that it may delay improvement without having the real facts to show where they need improvement. Data collection is tangible and works better to identify areas of weakness, especially using AI.

"For players, it just might be the last round where things did not go right. They just didn't have it that day for one part of their game. With the use of data, any coach can quickly see what's actually going on and then fast-track improvement in those areas. And the player can see the information and use that information for more relevant practice sessions on his own.

"There is a lot of technical data gathering for students at IOG. The Draw More Circles program provides benchmarks for college golfers, scratch golfers, PGA players, PGA top ten, and PGA winners, and more.

"As for the social golfer, it is easier to improve their game by just watching their technique and having them work on improving their technique. It's easier to improve them fast that way. When they get down to a 10 handicap or better, Circles is then very effective in quickly lowering their score.

"The benchmark or goals will set themselves once we get more information and data with the Circles program."

Remote coaching. I asked Guy about remote coaching. "Yes, we do remote coaching. Right now, one of my students is attending Duke University and if he has an issue, we get together online and go over it. I straighten it out and advise him on what to work on to solve the issue."

What Is the Draw More Circles Shot Data Program Exactly?

"The advance of technology is based on making it fit in so that you don't really even notice it, so it's part of everyday life."

-- Bill Gates

Most of us know birdies win tournaments, and you circle them on scorecards. I had read about the "Draw More Circles Shot Data Program" and was intrigued by what it does and how it works.

Hearing further that this program uses Artificial Intelligence (AI) and was very effective and produced real results fast, I was very curious to learn how Guy uses that and how it was developed.

I spoke with Craig Dixon, the Founder, and CEO of Draw More Circles. Craig is also Co-Director at IOG and travels a lot internationally.

When I thanked him for giving me his time for an interview, he said, "I am happy to help Guy anytime. He is a wonderful human being."

Craig began his love for golf when he was 12 years old and joined the NZPGA when he was 17. "I have a passion for helping people achieve their potential, and through golf, I'm fortunate to have the opportunity to work in an industry I'm extremely passionate about and work with motivated individuals."

Craig's career moved when the opportunity knocked on his door to work with exceptional players internationally. "And what we found was we couldn't support the players remotely as best as what we would have liked. That was our first step into data intelligence to remotely support players in optimizing their performance."

I made my appointment online with Craig to discuss the Circles Program that Guy, other IOG instructors, along with over 1000 coaches, across 32 countries use and integrate into their coaching. It was very easy to schedule online, and we used Zoom.

I wanted to know more about the Circles data intelligence platform as analytics are a golfer's friend in my view, so I asked Craig questions.

Q. Tell me how you became interested in analytics.

"I've worked to continually learn and develop myself to support players I work with. Part of my development is to surround myself with an exceptional team. In 2019 I was appointed the high-performance and big-data specialist for the Chinese Olympic golf team, and our results, since then, have blessed us with the opportunity to work with players on the

PGA, LPGA, LIV, and DP World Tour. We recognize golf is hard. In the development of Circles, we have a mechanism to gain insights into a player's game, optimize their training, and show how they can next play their course in statistically the lowest score.

"Pre-covid, we were busy. I was out of NZ for 258 days traveling with clients. When covid hit we took a step back and asked ourselves questions. What would happen if we provided our high-performance service and made it available to any golfer? We tested, and the results were incredible, so we developed Circles into what we expect to be the leader in performance insights for golf, globally.

"We are so proud to have a great team, and through the support of NZTE, Callaghan innovation, our shareholders, and advisors, we're excited about the future. We believe we can make a meaningful global impact within golf.

"When covid hit we took a step back and asked ourselves questions. What would happen if we provided our high-performance service and made it available to any golfer? We tested, and the results we're incredible, so we developed Circles

into what we expect to be the leader in performance insights for golf, globally. "

"We have thousands of players across 32 countries and through new features, we're expanding and growing. It's a beautiful opportunity to make golf development not just efficient but enjoyable."

Q. If any player wants to use the Circles program, can they try it out for free?

"Absolutely, we provide any player access to Circles for five rounds at no charge. We provide five rounds as this is the point our AI engages and provides players insight. During the five rounds, players can access personalized training plans and course strategy tools.

"There are a lot of statistic programs out there, and historically they provide information. They will give a player a lot of information, and that's great. However, that's just one of the pieces for success and results in performance. We take the information and curate it to drive meaningful action and lower scores.

"At Circles, we're dedicated to building the best product that creates the most value for our users.

"In our view, optimization has four key elements:

First, to optimize performance, you need to know where you're starting from.

Second, to optimize performance, you also need to know what you're aiming for.

For this, we have 20 benchmarks for players to choose from.

Third, to optimize performance, you need to know how to bridge any gaps between where you're starting from to what you're aiming for.

For this we use AI, and modeling to provide insights and focus areas.

Fourth, to optimize performance, you need to prepare in advance.

We provide the player's coach with the tools they need to help their students be successful. Our platform also provides the following features:

- Discussion document.

- Action plan.

- Periodization model.

- Practice plan.

- Course strategy.

- A regular cadence of analysis and communication.

Q. How about an example? Tell me about someone who used Circles and greatly improved.

Without any hesitation, Craig said, "Ronnie (Ruoning) Yin got on the LPGA tour and ranked 323rd in the World Golf Ranking. In only 8 months she improved huge amounts, and she is a very interesting story.

"She started instruction remotely and in person with IOG many years ago when she was a young teenager. She was a junior player when a team from the IOG went to China and worked with Auckland Unlimited and Education New Zealand.

"Guy and I provided educational and golf improvement services and went to China to look at players and award two scholarships. We looked for talented players and analyzed hundreds of them and selected two players for scholarships. Ronnie was one of those.

"Guy and I worked with her remotely for some time, and then she turned pro. She holds a Guinness World Record for winning her first three professional events.

"From there I worked with her using Circles when she wanted to join the LPGA Tour. We continued working with her remotely using Circles, and she eventually went through Q school. She wound up finishing second at Q school and got her LPGA card.

"She climbed to 143rd in World Golf Rankings and is playing on the LPGA Tour. And she's just one example.

Q. What about helping coaches?

"We also work with some of the world's best golf coaches who work with players on the PGA and LPGA Tours. They use Circles to find those little gold nuggets to lower scores. Circles helps the coach and player to train more optimally.

"Coaches get more organized with Circles. Just check out the videos on our website from three coaches."

Q. Yes. I saw the example case study by Richard Woodhouse, who was twice named Australian PGA Coach of the Year. (by the way, readers can watch the videos on the Draw More Circles.com website [41]). Tell me, what kind of players realize the best benefits from Circles?

"Circles is a product designed for elite players who are dedicated. But when we use the term elite player, we are referring to a player who is dedicated, motivated, and willing to put in time and effort into the journey of self-improvement. Circles is designed for those individuals."

Q. Tell me where Circles has become popular?

"Golf in China is growing rapidly. Eight years ago, there were only 125 junior registered golfers. Today they have over 72,000. The game is growing rapidly.

"Circles has a certification for coaches and have 300 certified coaches in China. It is a way to learn if the coach is the right fit for you or your child. We at Circles can connect a student to the most appropriate coach.

"Circles can be used remotely. You don't have to go to a local coach since you can use a remote coach. People are smart and busy and crunched for time. We can assist anyone globally to get connected with the right person that can get the best results for the player in the shortest time possible.

"In my view, there's a difference in having a lesson to feel better vs. getting better. Historically, players working with coaches remotely might send a video of their swing. The area of focus is often subjective. i.e., how a player is feeling about their game. Improvement, therefore, becomes player lead. Our intention is to provide the player and their coach with objective insights to dive into the exact areas that can help a player achieve their goal (objective vs. subjective).

"Circles gives that coach objective data to make informed decisions. And in my view, one of the key reasons why Circles brings so much value and improvement.

"At Circles, our product is about finding efficiencies; as a company, this is the philosophy we apply to everything."

I thanked Craig for his time and told him I was fascinated hearing about these innovations in golf instruction, especially for the low handicap golfers, and determined golfers who want to break the 70s or 80s.

The Creation Continues

"Champions know that success is inevitable; that there is no such thing as failure, only feedback. They know that the best way to forecast the future is to create it."

--Michael J. Gelb

Guy and IOG continue creating outstanding golfers playing at the highest levels. Here are just a few of them.

Bohyun Park. Guy coached Bohyun from when she was around 11 years old for 5 years. She had lessons and practiced 2 to 3 days a week at the IOG Center. She's presently playing on a scholarship and in her sophomore year at the University of Texas. She won First Team All-American honors as a freshman. [42]

Fox Sports reported on Bohyun Park. "Bohyun is a world class golfer and a world-class human being" and "has too many records to list." Some of her statistics are that she had 31 wins out of 33 events and won two state Texas Championships – one by 24 strokes and many more accomplishments.

Fox News Report did a 7-minute report which is on YouTube (link is referenced) after she was named a "freshman sensation" and made First Team All-American in the U.S. [43]

"I caddied for Bohyun in regional tournaments around Auckland and used that information to focus on her weaknesses. She was doing well and winning, and it was like coaching Lydia - she was a little girl competing against adults. And she moved up the rankings in New Zealand without a lot of financial support, and it was a hurdle again just like Lydia."

Bohyun and her father practiced and played at Gulf Harbour Golf Club. She knew Lydia so well that Lydia even gave her a set of her golf clubs to help her along her expensive journey.

The University of Texas Golf is one of the strongest NCAA Division I golf teams in the U.S. Jordan Spieth and Scottie Scheffler are alumni.

Golf News (featuring the latest women's golf news) tweeted, "I watched Bohyunniee's (@bohynniee) progress when she was living here in New Zealand. A family that has dedicated all to give their daughter the best opportunity to fulfill her dream. Having Guy Wilson as her coach was a major influence, as is Lydia Ko."

A video of Bohyun's fascinating golf journey on the Longhorn Network is in the Reference at the back of this book (see References endnote 44). [44] Her story is magical.

Her father and Bohyun continue to reach out to Guy and keep in touch. She and her father practiced at Gulf Harbour Country Club where Lydia played and practiced as well.

Bohyun Park (Picture courtesy of Guy Wilson)

Lin Xi Yu. Lin Xi Yu (Xi Yu Lin) is a former student coached by Gareth Winslow. She is playing the LPGA Tour and is ranked 13th in Rolex Women's' World Golf Rankings.

Gareth, the former national coach of the Chinese Women's Team, was happy to see his former student Lin Xi Yu fire a final round 65 to secure a second-place finish at the inaugural LPGA Tour's Kroger Queen City Championship event. She was just one shot out of the lead.

Lita Guo. Lita trained with IOG for several years and carved her path to go to one the most major Universities in the U.S. She graduated from Harvard with a double major in economics and East Asian study.

She was captain of Harvard's Women's golf team during her senior year.

She played on the New Zealand National team for two years and ranked in the Top 30 in the AJGA and ranked No. 1 on New Zealand's Women's Order of Merit for Golf. She was a Bronze medalist on the Australian Youth Olympics Mixed team and had many more achievements.

Ruoning (Ronni) Yin. "Ronni was one of the two candidates that were given scholarships to come to New Zealand. She and her family spent a month here and her family loved it.

We ran the program the next year and Ronni won it again," Guy explained.

"A couple of times I went to China to work with her and other players. I would stay there for 3 weeks and coach every day. That was less expensive than having them come to NZ.

"I was hosted at a golf facility in different provinces and taught golf every day. Then, unfortunately, the pandemic stopped it."

Ronni was a winner of IOG's Next World Number 1 (NW#1) search in 2016 and 2017 in China. By doing so, she earned a trip to Auckland.

She turned professional in 2020, primarily playing on the China LPGA Tour.

She finished in the top 3 at the LPGA Qualifying Tournament Stage II with a four-day total of 275 (-13).

She won her first three events in a row on the China LPGA Tour as a professional in 2020, which was a record for the Chinese tour, and she had six top-10s on the China LPGA Tour during the 2020 season.

Before that, she won nine titles in 2019 as a junior amateur and was ranked as high as 64th in the World Amateur Golf Rankings.

She won the 2019 Buick LPGA, and a year later, she won the 2020 China LPGA's (CLPGA) Zhuhai Hollywood Mansion Challenge.

She earned her LPGA card in December 2021 and is doing extremely well on the LPGA tour winning her first tournament.

Guy and Ronni Yin (Picture courtesy of IOG)

Guy continues creating excellence. Ronni recently was victorious in the LPGA DIO Implant LPGA Los Angeles Open on April 2, 2023, taking home $262,500 (first place)! [45]

Fiona Xu. Fiona started at the IOG Center around 2015 and now is 17 years old. She lived near the IOG site in Ellerslie.

When she started IOG lessons she had a single-digit handicap in her teens. "We taught her more on her technique and fine-tuned it and pushed her toward tournaments and tournaments overseas."

In 2019, she won the American Junior Golf Championship. In 2020, she won the New Zealand amateur championship and the 2022 Australian Amateur championship. [46] Golf Australia reported she played like "she was in cruise control." [47]

Fiona also finished in the top 10 against professionals in the Australian Open in late 2022 and is ranked 35th in the Official Woman's World Golf Rankings.

Jimmy Zheng. "Jimmy came to IOG and spent 6 years with us. His goal was to get a scholarship. He accomplished that and is playing on a scholarship at Duke University, one of the best golf teams in the US.

As a sophomore last year, Jimmy was named to the All-ACC Academic Team. He shot his season low of 64 in the first round of the Old Town Club Collegiate and recorded eight rounds in the 60s, including back-to-back rounds (66, 69) in the second and third rounds of the Rod Myers Invitational.

He had six eagles during the season, a team high.

Jimmy Zheng (Picture courtesy of IOG)

Jimmy was mentioned in an article by Golf Channel as being one of the top 30 golfers in the United States. [48]

He stays in contact with Guy who occasionally coaches him remotely if Jimmy has an urgent issue, and Jimmy travels back to NZ during the bigger University breaks for some one-on-one time with Guy.

Stephen Liu. "The entire IOG team coached Stephen for 6 years. He came in twice a week except when he was playing in events.

"He traveled to the US to see how he would compete in three tournaments and finished in 8th place at the highly competitive AJGA Junior Open at Palouse Ridge Golf Club in Washington.

"The next week he finished in 3rd place at the AJGA Great LIFE Junior Challenge by Sanford Health.

"In the final tournament Stephen, on a very difficult course with extremely heavy rough around the fairways and greens, he finished 5 under par and won the tournament."

Stephen continues to compete weekly and is on the Premier golf team at Macleans College in Auckland.

Steven uses the Circles program and says, "Circles helps me practice more efficiently as I know what I'm doing will translate to lower scores."

Jerry Ren. As a child, Jerry played at the Gulf Harbour Country Club in Gulf Harbour, New Zealand around the same time Lydia played there. They knew each other well.

"I worked with Jerry for two to three years. We would work with him here at IOG from the time he was 15 years old. His goal was to get a scholarship." Guy said.

Jerry did that by getting a scholarship at an NCAA Division I University in Georgia, and he also earned a Bachelor of Business Administration, majoring in Finance and Economics (Summa Cum Laude), and earned a Master of Finance degree at the University of Auckland.

Sarah Li. Guy sees similarities between Lydia and NOW ten-year-old Sarah Li who is one of his students who is progressing very well. Sarah already has a hole-in-one on a 120-meter hole.

Sarah Li scores a hole-in-one on a 120-meter hole (Picture courtesy of IOG.)

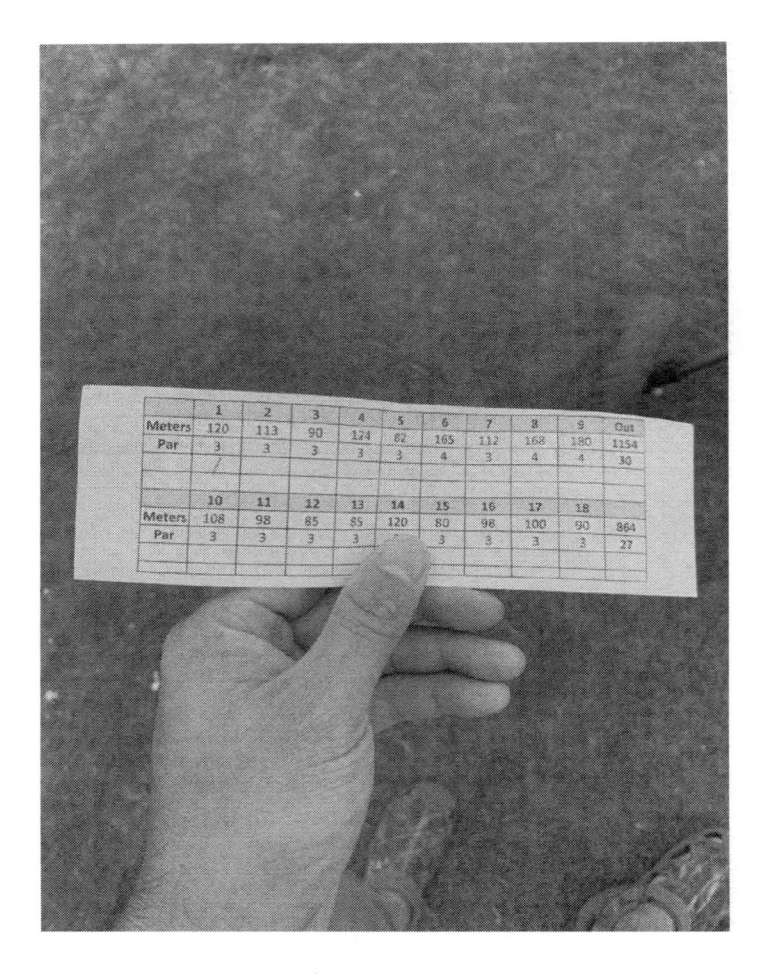

Sarah's Scorecard 1st hole – 1 (Picture courtesy of IOG)

Sarah wants to play in the LPGA and worldwide tournaments. Guy noticed Sarah had the same smile and enthusiasm that Lydia had.

TVNZ's 1 NEWS did a feature and an article on this amazing little 10-year-old, calling her the "Golf Prodigy Following Eerily Similar Path as Idol Lydia Ko." [49]

One of Lydia's achievements was winning the Pupuke Golf Course Women's Club Championship when she was 11 years old. Sarah went to the Pupuke Golf Course Clubhouse and saw Lydia's name in gold on the Women's Club Champion's plaque.

Guy told Sarah if she won, she would get her name in gold too. She decided to play in it.

You might be wondering why the largest Television Station in New Zealand took the time to do this feature on Sarah. Well, little Sarah came out on top, winning the Women's Club 3-round Championship by an incredible 39 strokes! And that's an incredible margin – more than Tiger when he was in his prime!

Guy uses the latest technology in teaching Sarah including the shot data Circles program when she plays a golf course.

Sarah has developed an excellent golf swing far beyond her years and looking forward to a bright future and enjoying it all on the way.

10-year-old Sarah Li (Picture courtesy of IOG).

Creating Excellence

"Better than a thousand days of diligent study is one day with a great teacher."

>   *-- Japanese Proverb*

Guy loves coaching and is highly professional, knowledgeable, dedicated, and passionate about it and continues creating and guiding golfers to play their best and enjoy the journey.

He gave Lydia a strong foundation and continues to create excellent golfers who obtain university scholarships and compete professionally at the highest levels.

He builds good character and teaches them the right attitude to enjoy a sport that can be so unrewarding and frustrating to so many. And that certainly is invaluable to whichever path one chooses in life.

Lydia has been known for her pleasant disposition on the course and other LPGA players have said she is an enjoyable person to play with. YouGov is an international research data and analytics company headquartered in London, and through their polling and research found that Lydia is one of the highest-ranked Tour golfers in popularity. [50]

As Guy explained before, "Lydia wasn't ever proud of beating the others. You know the types that beat you and rub it in your face? When she was a youngster, and adults were beaten by a little girl and were feeling bad about losing, she would encourage them and tell them 'Come on you can do this.'"

Guy gives his students a strong foundation that will last a lifetime as well as instills a positive and wonderful attitude in children to have their whole lives.

Arnold Palmer said golf can be "deceptively simple and endlessly complicated."

Einstein said true genius is "taking the complex and making it simple."

And it takes, even more, to make what's complicated and sometimes frustrating so simple that even a child can understand and excel at the game.

Perhaps the subtitle of this book should be, *"The Genius Behind Lydia Ko and More Stars."*

Afterword

Arnold Palmer said golf can be "deceptively simple and endlessly complicated."

Einstein said true genius is "taking the complex and making it simple." And it takes, even more, to make what's complicated and sometimes frustrating so simple that even a child can understand and excel at the game.

At first, Guy seemed to me a quiet and confident person -- one of those who sits peacefully in the back of the classroom calmly observing all the loud and obnoxious people who know nothing yet always have something to say about everything.

I was continually amazed at his extensive knowledge and answers and his ability to consistently come up with precise, complete, and in-depth answers to anything I asked during our many meetings.

This is not only my opinion but also the view of the many excellent and outstanding people surrounding him.

I hope you someday get a chance to meet and learn from him. He's a remarkable person, and I enjoyed the experience. I understand now why Lydia and the other up-and-coming stars he coaches or has coached are doing so well.

More about Guy Wilson

Guy Wilson is the Director of Instruction for the Institute of Golf. His instruction provides a pivotal role in educating, inspiring and assessing the ongoing performance of his players.

Guy's holistic approach to coaching makes him an ideal instructor for any player looking to take their game to the next level.

The Institute of Golf's methodology and Guy's knowledge and passion for coaching combined will ensure his pupils have great success in reaching their desired goals.

His Qualifications include:

- AAA Class member status of the New Zealand Professional Golfers Association
- Trackman Master Certified
- Level Two TPI Golf Professional Certified
- Level One TPI Fitness Instructor Certified
- Level Two TPI Junior Instructor Certified
- Certificate in Anatomy and Physiology
- FlightScope Certified (3D Doppler radar)
- Certified in Crossfit Olympic Weightlifting
- Level Two K Vest Certified (3D motion sensors)

Guy has been named by Golf Digest as one of the 2020 Top 80 Instructors in the world. He also was a Halberg Awards Coach of the Year Finalist in 2014, and coached many highly successful national and international players.

His instruction has led students to win the US Women's Amateur Championship, the LPGA Canadian Open, the NSW

Open on the WPGA Tour (formerly known as the ALPG Tour), the LET New Zealand Women's Open, the Australian Women's Amateur Championship, the New Zealand Women's Amateur Championship, and many others.

About the Author

Lawyer, businessman, world traveler, private pilot, and founder of Team Golfwell Books, Bruce Miller has written over 50 books with several Amazon bestsellers.

He spends his days writing, studying, and constantly learning about the astounding, unexpected, and amazing events happening in the world today while exploring the brighter side of life and playing golf, of course.

He created the Facebook group "Golf Jokes and Stories" with 300,000+ members and growing.

He's a member of the Independent Book Publishers Association.

References

[1] Palm Springs Life, https://www.palmspringslife.com/seven-lakes-country-club-modernism/

[2] Golf Channel, https://www.golfchannel.com/article/grill-room/day-golf-president-ford-makes-ace-fedex-st-jude

[3] Independent, i.e., https://www.independent.ie/world-news/and-finally/which-former-us-president-made-a-hole-in-one-on-the-golf-course-37938782.html

[4] Youngest Winners in LPGA History, Golf Compendium, https://www.golfcompendium.com/2021/11/youngest-winners-lpga-tour.html#:~:text=Lydia%20Ko

[5] Ibid.

[6] The New York Times, Karen Clouse, "The Girl Wonder of Golf", Karen Clouse, https://www.nytimes.com/2012/09/13/sports/golf/lydia-ko-acts-like-a-teenager-but-golfs-like-a-veteran.html

[7] Ibid.

[8] Humor Boosts Retention, Sarah Henderson, March 31, 2015, Edutopia, https://www.edutopia.org/blog/laughter-learning-humor-boosts-retention-sarah-henderson

[9] "Laughter is the Best Medicine", Help Guide, Your trusted non-profit guide to health and wellness, December 5, 2022, https://www.helpguide.org/articles/mental-health/laughter-is-the-best-medicine.htm

[10] Ibid.

[11] Eutopia, George Lucas Educational Foundation, "Laughter and Learning: Humor Boosts Retention," https://www.edutopia.org/blog/laughter-learning-humor-boosts-retention-sarah-henderson

[12] Ibid.

[13] Official LPGA Statistics,
https://www.lpga.com/news/2022/kpmg-performance-insights-best-insights-of-the-2022-lpga-tour-season#:~:text=16.8%25%20came%20on%20tee%20shots,shots%20in%20the%202022%20season, and
https://www.lpga.com/news/2022/kpmg-performance-insights-best-insights-of-the-2022-lpga-tour-season#

[14] Official LPGA Statistics, https://www.lpga.com/statistics/short-game/putting-average?year=2022

[15] "Signs of Negative Energy", WebMD clinical staff,
https://www.webmd.com/balance/signs-negative-energy

[16] Ibid.

[17] Wikipedia, Bungee jumping,
https://en.wikipedia.org/wiki/Bungee_jumping

[18] "Lydia Ko - Golfer - On Close Up in New Zealand with Coach Guy Wilson." https://youtu.be/1JjiSkEl6Vk

[19] Ibid.

[20] "Golfing in New Zealand: Lydia Ko's favourite fairways"
Australian Senior Golfer,
https://australianseniorgolfer.com.au/19335/golfing-in-new-zealand-lydia-kos-favourite-fairways/

[21] Lydia Ko & Sir David Levene at the Outward-Bound Charity Golf Day, Sports Inc. TV & Events, YouTube,
https://www.youtube.com/watch?v=noJYJMXzeAM

[22] Ibid.

[23] PLOS ONE, "Associations between organized sport participation and mental health difficulties: Data from over 11,000 US children and adolescents",
https://journals.plos.org/plosone/article?id=10.1371/journal.pone.0268583

[24] Ibid.

[25] Ibid.

[26] IOG Facebook, https://fb.watch/jcQ78KtWlb/

[27] Wikipedia, Lydia Ko, https://en.wikipedia.org/wiki/Lydia_Ko

[28] Ibid.

[29] Ibid.

[30] Ibid.

[31] Ibid.

[32] Ibid.

[33] Reuters News, https://www.reuters.com/article/us-golf-lpga-ko-idUSBRE99R0LF20131028

[34] Ibid.

[35] "Teen LPGA star Lydia Ko leaves coach she started with at age 5", LA Times, by David Wharton, https://www.latimes.com/sports/la-xpm-2013-dec-23-la-sp-sn-lpga-lydia-ko-coach-guy-wilson-20131223-story.html

[36] USA Today, December 23, 2013, https://www.usatoday.com/story/sports/golf/2013/12/23/teen-golfer-lydia-ko-splits-with-coach-of-11-years/4173375/

[37] IOG Director of Instruction Guy Wilson combines fancy face technology with Trackman technology. Facebook IOG, https://fb.watch/jd6mBzX4I6/

[38] Ibid.

[39] TrackMan, Wikipedia, https://en.wikipedia.org/wiki/TrackMan

[40] CoachNow, https://coachnow.io/

[41] Draw More Circles helpful videos, https://help.drawmorecircles.com/en/collections/3053250-helpful-videos

[42] Texas Women's Golf, Twitter, https://twitter.com/TexasWGolf/status/1533873950891155464

43 Bally Sports Network, Twitter, Fox Sports, https://twitter.com/BallySportsSW/status/1371540538743164929?s=24&fbclid=IwAR2dtO_O0QpRQnVvdkkDtpJN6hRzH5qi8cUp7vFeQttx779CzapQGTkcDhE

44 Texas Women's Golf, Twitter, https://twitter.com/TexasWGolf/status/1533873950891155464

45 Prize money DIO LPGA LA Open, Yahoo Sports, https://sports.yahoo.com/dio-implant-la-open-purse-202542267.html#

46 "McKinney (men's title) and Xu (women's title) take Australian Amateur titles, Golf Australia, https://www.golfaustralia.com.au/fiona-xu

47 Ibid.

48 "Men's college golf: Spring power rankings, conference previews", by Brentley Romine, Golf Channel, https://www.golfchannel.com/news/mens-college-golf-spring-power-rankings-conference-previews?fbclid=IwAR3GT2nG_abK1_Cdp_a98CWy03RICRdLjeQzzFOzchmEOYoJQrzuelLsvLc

49 1 News, "Golf prodigy following eerily similar path as idol Lydia Ko," https://www.1news.co.nz/2022/05/31/golf-prodigy-following-eerily-similar-path-as-idol-lydia-ko/

50 The Most Popular Contemporary Golfers (Q4 2022), YouGov, https://today.yougov.com/ratings/sports/popularity/contemporary-golfers/all

Printed in Great Britain
by Amazon

d1d0dd07-36ca-4032-b350-fddb451fe1c9R01